COLLEGE COMES SOONER THAN YOU THINK!

COLLEGE COMES SOONER THAN YOU INK!

The College Planning Guide for High School Students and Their Families

By Jill M. Reilly and Bonnie D. Featherstone

Creators of the Individualized College Planning Workshops

THE CAREER PRESS
62 Beverly Rd., PO Box 34
Hawthorne, NJ 07507
1-800-CAREER-1

College Comes Sooner Than You Think
ISBN 0-934829-24-1, $9.95

This book may be ordered by mail or phone directly from the publisher. To order by mail, please include price noted above plus $2.00 shipping per book ordered. (New Jersey residents please add 6% sales tax.) Send to: The Career Press Inc., 62 Beverly Rd., PO Box 34, Hawthorne, NJ 07507. Or call **Toll-Free 1-800-CAREER-1** to order using your VISA or Mastercard or for further information on all books published or distributed by The Career Press.

Bookstore distribution by Williamson Publishing, Charlotte, VT.

Illustrated by Steve Fasen & Gary Fasen

DEDICATION

To Kevin Featherstone,
who in his innocence started it all.

To Elizabeth, Joseph and Heather Reilly,
who have yet to endure our enthusiasm and tenacity.

To Robert Featherstone and Patrick Reilly,
who because of their encouragement and support only recently realized what they had wrought upon themselves.

And To Students and Parents,
who have the curiosity and courage to plan for the future together.

With love,
B. F. & J. R.
1987

ACKNOWLEDGMENTS

Our sincere thanks to the following people for their insightful comments about the manuscript: • Jon M. Nicholson, Dean of Admissions, Carleton College • Howard Hall, Principal, Burnsville HS • Barbara Gall, Counselor, Burnsville HS • Gerard Ackerman, Asst. Superintendant, Burnsville HS • Joseph A. Karulak, Dean, Rosemont HS • John Hanson, Director of Secondary Education, ISD #196 • Charles Erickson, Counselor, Apple Valley HS • Jack Holm, Asst. Superintendent, Inver Grove Heights School District • Sandra Olson, Career Center Coordinator, Simley HS • Karla Lankford • Fred P. Meyer, Assistant Principal, Middleville Jr. HS • Diane Webber, Miami University of Ohio • Bruce Cappels • Ed Rimkus, Gifted Coordinator, Spring Lake Park Schools • Raymond T. Brett • Dr. Robert Tschirke, Superintendant, Littleton (CO) School District • Donald McGuire, Dakota County (MN) Technical Institute • Patricia Roberts • John Galland, Student • The Richard Beckman Family • Kay Fecke, Gifted Coordinator and Parent • Mary Kuske, Financial Planner, Judith Brown & Associates • Gary Kubat, Editor, *This Week Newspapers* • The 1987 Mentor Connection Class • Our *Individualized College Planning Workshop* Families. • Thanks to Joel Anderson, Proactive Counselor for the Gifted, St. Louis Park Schools, for sharing his "Value Pac" with us (and allowing us to reprint it)

TABLE OF CONTENTS

PART 2 THE COLLEGE SEARCH

PART 3 CHARTING YOUR PROGRESS

INTRODUCTION

How This Book Will Help You

Families often spend hours shopping for the right used car for their son or daughter. Teenager, mom, dad, brothers, sisters, even grandparents, all have opinions, usually contradictory, on style, color, economy, sound systems...and how to get it all for under $3,000.

Unfortunately when it comes to "shopping" for an education, few families take as much time "kicking the tires" of a college education, certainly a more important and longer lasting investment. And there are even more contradictory opinions and desires, many of which go unexplored, undiscussed, unresolved.

Choosing a college isn't *that* different from getting the right used car. As with any major purchase, you need to agree on the "features" you want and then "shop around," finding the right college at the right price. In other words, you need to become choosy college consumers.

This volume, the first book aimed at both students and their parents searching for that elusive "right" college, will help each and all of you sort out your options, identify the areas of compromise you need to discuss and develop the coordinated strategy that will satisfy each of your desires.

Why is all this necessary? Grasping at too many options or struggling after the wrong ones will just add to everyone's confusion. And make it less likely that the college you choose will be an appropriate one.

This guide will help you (students and parents and other family members) define your options, recognize your priorities and keep your energies focused on the choices that fit your mutual objectives. By following the advice and plans in this guide, you can be confident that you have blazed a logical path to the best choice for everyone. Just remember—there may be a number of "best" choices; there is no single *perfect* choice. Rather, you will probably identify several suitable colleges that will fulfill your needs.

Does it surprise you to think you can be as choosy about a college education as you would be with a 1978 Plymouth? Well, you *can* be choosy. Colleges are not just in business, they are *big* business. All of them—from the smallest liberal arts school to the most prestigious, ivy-covered halls—*need* students to *stay* in business. A qualified student has the means to get to and get into many different colleges. You—students and parents—are the consumers who pay the college's bills. So don't feel guilty about asking questions or inquiring into the policies or operations of the colleges where you might apply. You will assist in the financing of the institution you choose. Don't be afraid to ask yourselves how *your* efforts and *your* money can best be invested.

College really does come sooner than you think. And the planning process is probably more involved and time-consuming that you think.

When should you start to plan for college? By the time the student reaches middle school or junior high, there should be some awareness of and interest in education beyond high school. While the college planning process should begin by the end of junior high, it *must* begin by the fall of the student's sophomore year of high school.

STUDENT

You first must understand yourself and, as a key part of that self-examination process, *your* needs and wants for education after high school. Too often, many of you worry: "What college will take me?" "What college can I afford?" "What college is prestigious enough?"

Remember: This is a two-way street. First, *identify what you have to offer a college.* Then research *what a particular college has to offer you.* This double-edged approach will enable you to choose a school where you have the best opportunity to succeed, given your talents and limitations.

Planning for college is also a perfect opportunity to establish mature communication channels with your parents. Although you may feel you should be making this decision by yourself (after all, it's *your* education, not theirs), try to appreciate how much more experience they have had in the world. Even if they haven't been through the college selection process with your brothers or sisters (or to college themselves), they can offer you some sound advice and donate their time and energy organizing and keeping your search on track.

PARENTS

Students can obtain information and counseling through their schools. But *your* involvement in the planning process is critical. By being involved right from the start, you can help your student systematically plan high school courses and extracurricular activities to reach the goal you've all identified. And you'll allow yourself more time to deal with a most complex issue—time that can only lead to better and better-thought-out decisions.

You may wonder, with some discomfort, just how to provide support and information on college and career guidance if you know little or nothing about the subjects. Whatever your own college experiences, even if they're nonexistent, the biggest and best contributions you can make are advice (both when asked and even, sometimes, when unasked) and your precious time and organizational efforts. *All* will be essential contributions to the college search process.

BOTH

Does the task sound overwhelming? Take heart! You're not alone. This book has been written to help students and parents work together to gather and organize the information necessary to arrive at quality choices. You'll learn how to utilize this information for the best interests of the student, eliminate the mystery of the college selection process and reduce the stress on everyone that, unfortunately, comes with the territory.

How To Use This Guide

This book is a result of our personal involvement in college planning, the college search, the application process, financial planning and campus visits. During our college planning workshops, we have worked with traditional and single-parent families, with parents rich and poor, white-collar and blue-collar, college graduates and non-college graduates. And their sons and daughters, just as varied, just as confused. Because of these broad experiences, we can lead you through the minefields of choices all of you will face in the college planning process.

In addition to the obvious concerns—researching colleges and getting accepted to the one(s) you want—the primary focus of this guide is to *understand the needs of the individual student*. But, in order to know that student, *parents' visions and values* are included in the process.

We begin with exercises to help *all* planners. (Planners are anyone assisting the student—grandmas and grandpas, counselors, uncles or friends can all be important ingredients in the student's search for an appropriate college.) Each planner needs to identify the particular dreams and hopes *he or she* has for the student's education, then move into organizing records and information in preparation for the application process. Succeeding chapters cover preparation for tests, applying for financial aid, organizing campus visits and comparing and rating colleges.

Several planning tools included at the end of this book will need to be used at various points of your planning. Chapter 12—a Month-By-Month Planning Calendar—gives you an overview of the college planning tasks involved in each year of high school. Refer to this Calendar now—and as you continue from task to task—to keep everything in perspective and stay on schedule.

Chapter 13—What's The Plan?—allows you to identify many essential tasks and keep track of who's responsible for completing them and when.

The final chapter is a helpful compendium of resources for information on topics related to the college planning process.

You've probably already noticed our peculiar habit of labeling subsections for **Students**, **Parents** or **Both**. Essential information for each group is included in these sections. Although all the contents can certainly be read by all planners, the subdivisions make it easier for everyone to find important information, directions and suggestions directed just to *them*.

Use this volume as your college planning workbook. Write in it. It will help. And you *will* make it through! We've survived and had fun. So can you!

counselors, parents, or friends can all be important [illegible] in [illegible] as soon as [illegible] appropriate colleges, each planner needs to identify the particular programs and hopes [illegible] for the student's education, then move into organizing resources and information for preparation for the application process. Succeeding chapters cover preparation for tests, applying for financial aid, organizing campus visits, and choosing and paying for college.

[illegible] planning tools included at the end of the book will be used as needed at various points of your planning. Chapter [illegible] Month-by-Month Planning [illegible] overview of the college planning tasks involved in each year of high school [illegible] now [illegible] you [illegible]

The [illegible] What's [illegible] many [illegible] tests and deadlines of why [illegible] for [illegible] and when.

The [illegible] that [illegible] related [illegible]

[illegible]

[illegible] what college planning is all about. What [illegible] And you will make it through! We've [illegible] to help you.

PART ONE

Getting To Know Each Other

CHAPTER ONE

Just Imagine!

BOTH

In the Introduction, we asked students to begin their college planning by thinking about what they have to offer a college and by trying to understand what they as individuals want from a college. We know this is a tall order. Because of the difficulty of resolving these emerging issues, parents' (and other planners') advice can really help and encourage the student. The following activity will get all of you off to an excellent start in knowing yourselves and knowing the student. Just relax and use your imagination.

Each planner in the family has unique dreams and desires for the student's college life, due to that individual's personality type, parents' or student's past experiences, interests, values, family history, even the influence of television, movies or books. While Mom imagines that her daughter will live in a sorority house and spend most of her time in a social whirl, the daughter imagines herself hard at work in the chemistry lab and living in an off-campus apartment.

Before they can negotiate a plan of action, all planners need to become clearly aware of their unique visions for the student.

An excellent foundation for learning to communicate about college plans is to share your dreams. Simply listening to one another's fantasies will identify some clear goals almost immediately and help everyone face realities (some unpleasant) far more quickly.

For example, one family was surprised to find they all shared the same dream: their son would play soccer on a scholarship at an academically strong school in the Midwest. Having quickly identified a common goal made it easier (and allowed more time) for this family to figure out how to accomplish it together.

In another situation, a father "saw" his daughter sitting in a Queen Anne wing chair reading Shakespeare. The ivy-covered walls of the Gothic buildings seen through her dorm window clearly described the type of prestigious, Northeastern school he imagined his daughter would attend.

The daughter, on the other hand, saw herself in a warm, sunny environment, wearing shorts and riding with friends down palm-lined streets.

As they discussed their individual dreams, the father quickly realized that *his* dream had little to do with his daughter. It was based on his own regret at not having taken better advantage of his own education at an Ivy League school. It was apparent his daughter clearly *didn't* want that kind of education or institution. Prior to their discussion, there had been (not surprisingly!) lots of disagreements. After they shared their dreams, the family was more open to compromising and working together to make *their* dream come true.

Identifying Your Own Dreams

At this point we suggest each of you consider for a moment not what anyone else wants for this student, but what *you alone* truly want. We also suggest that you refrain from considering whether your vision is a realistic one. Just imagine. You'll need to sort out reality soon enough.

Relax, dream your own spontaneous dream, and write it down. Just imagine...

STUDENT

JUST IMAGINE...

THIS EXERCISE IS DESIGNED TO HELP YOU TO UNDERSTAND *YOUR OWN* DREAMS AND HOPES. THINK ONLY ABOUT WHAT *YOU* BELIEVE IS BEST FOR YOU—

NOT OTHER PEOPLE'S EXPECTATIONS. WRITE DOWN YOUR ANSWERS WITHOUT DISCUSSING THEM WITH ANYONE ELSE.

You have been in college for a few months. Let your imagination run free. Think of the ideal college for you. Write in the space provided what you see in your mind as you read each question.

Where are you? What school or what building?

What are you doing?

What is important to you about this college?

Where is it located?

What are you studying there?

If you could do anything else at this school besides taking course work, what would it be?

Look back at what you've written, review your dreams. Which are realistic, which sheer fantasy? The following materials and activities will help you sort out and decide what you want and need. Give yourself time to complete this book. It's worth the effort. We promise!

PARENTS

JUST IMAGINE...

THIS EXERCISE IS DESIGNED TO HELP YOU UNDERSTAND *YOUR OWN* DREAMS AND HOPES FOR THE STUDENT. THINK ABOUT WHAT *YOU* WANT FOR THE STUDENT. LATER THERE WILL BE MANY OPPORTUNITIES FOR YOU TO HEAR AND UNDERSTAND THE DREAMS AND DESIRES OF OTHER PLANNERS AND THE STUDENT. PARENTS AND OTHER PLANNERS SHOULD COMPLETE THIS ACTIVITY WITHOUT DISCUSSING IT WITH ANYONE ELSE—INCLUDING SPOUSES.

The student has been in college for a few months. Let your imagination run free. Think of the college *you* want the student to attend and write in the space provided what you see in your mind as you read each question.

Where is the student? What school or what building?

What is he or she doing?

What is important to you about this college?

Where is it located?

What is the student studying there?

If the student could do anything else at this school in additon to taking course work, what would you want it to be?

As a parent or student supporter, you must be clear about what *your* dreams are for the student as well as identifying how and where the student's dreams differ from everyone else's (including your own). This, we have found, is one of the thorniest problems parents encounter when assisting in planning the student's future education.

Please review what you have "imagined" and ask yourself: "Have I dreamed my own dream here, my spouse's or my child's?" Use this exercise to understand what *you alone* dream for the student. Your dreams can offer tremendous support and provide the student with a different perspective and (you hope) perhaps some "food for thought."

This is just a beginning exercise, one that hopefully will open some initial channels of communication between the student and other interested planners. In the next chapter, you'll get involved in a far more detailed analysis of just what everyone wants...and how to deal with the contradictions that will inevitably surface.

CHAPTER TWO

For Students: Who Am I?

You've had a chance to dream. Now it's time to identify the "real" you.

It's an exciting, challenging and, sometimes, scary idea. But no matter how such self-evaluation scares you, don't skip this exercise—it's the most important in the book and the basis for much of the planning you and your parents must do.

There are a number of different ways to approach the following exercise. On a normal day you fall, no doubt, somewhere in between the following two logical extremes:

1. "I think this whole idea is stupid, but we bought the book, so I suppose I should do it."

2. "Maybe I am as interesting as my parents, teachers and friends think I am. For once I can get myself down on paper without being embarrassed about what I write or being evaluated by someone else."

The purpose of completing the "Who Am I?" exercise is to help you analyze *yourself*. You will begin this self-discovery process by identifying your academic strengths and weaknesses, subject likes and dislikes. They might well be different —just because you do well in a given subject doesn't mean you particularly like it. It's important you pay as much attention to areas you *like* as you do to those at which you excel.

"Who Am I?" will also help you assess the value of your extracurricular activities and the time commitment you have made over the years to develop specific skills and talents. These skills and interests may very well be important considerations in your college shopping and selection. If you definitely want to continue a particular activity, you should make it a priority in the selection process. It's as important to *you* as the school's academic offerings.

Different people learn best in different environments and with different teaching techniques. Current educational research shows that your needs for light, sound, food, visual aids, and hearing, reading or writing down information are unique. Some people can't concentrate on their studies while music's playing; others almost seem to *require* music to concentrate at all! So, finally, this exercise will help you identify how you prefer to learn, an essential step in pinpointing your individual learning style. By becoming cognizant of the various elements of your own, unique learning style, you'll have more specific requirements to include in your college shopping equation.

Even if you still think this exercise seems silly, you'll be amazed at some of the results. There will be areas where you and your parents agree 100 percent—often things you *never* would have expected you'd agree on. Then, of course, there'll be areas of 180-degree disagreement—some of those might surprise you, too.

There are no right or wrong answers to any of the questions in this exercise; if you and your parents radically disagree on the answers to particular questions, that just points out the need for more discussion. So if your answers differ markedly from those of your parents or other planners, don't be alarmed; just keep communications open.

This exercise—and the one for your parents and other planners that follows in the next chapter—has been designed to tease you into understanding each other. The discussion that should follow their completion will give all of you an opportunity to confront misconceptions that you may never have even known about.

One dad, for example, thought his daughter, obviously an excellent student, spent all her time studying and that studying was what she most liked to do. He was worried she studied *too* much and wasn't taking advantage of the extracurricular activities he thought were also important. Wrong. Dad worked late, rarely returning home before 7:00 p.m. By that time his daughter *was* studying, but she had spent the rest of the afternoon enjoying her leisure activities. The daughter fully intended to include these activities in her college life. The family agreed, and the discussion eased Dad's anxiety about how much his daughter studied.

This exercise may be a challenge if you and your parents aren't used to sitting down and talking on a one-to-one, adult-to-adult basis; but as challenging as it may get, it will definitely be a very rewarding experience for all of you. If you've never done so, it will force you to relate to your parents as an adult with thoughts, plans, dreams, and desires all your own. And, of course, force *them* to see you that way. By opening up to them, you'll all understand each other better and find the whole selection process will run more smoothly.

How To Do This Exercise

1. Complete the Who Am I? questions. Work alone. NO FRIENDS!

2. Schedule a definite* meeting time with your parents to listen to what they wrote on their sheets and to have them listen to yours. This meeting may take one hour or more. It may even require a series of meetings over a few nights.

3. Ask *clarifying* questions only, those intended to ensure that you understand what the speaker is saying. For example:

“Mom, are you saying that you expect I will enjoy my math assignments more than my English assignments?” Let everybody speak their piece and try to really understand what each person is saying. Save your comments and discussion for later.

4. If, at this meeting, you are having a good time sharing with your parents, spend as much time as you'd like. This kind of communication doesn't always happen between teenagers and parents, so take advantage of it!

5. While you are listening to your parents, write notes about the areas where you agree and disagree (using the sheets provided at the end of chapter four).

6. During the first meeting, or at another time you and your parents have scheduled*, discuss the areas where you and your parents agree. That's the easy part. List all of these on the "We Agree" Sheet on page 51.

*NOTE: This means choosing a day and time on the calendar. This is important business and the scheduled time should be considered inviolable—it takes priority over unexpected phone calls or dates, yours *and* your parents.

7. Then list areas where your answers differ on the "Up For Debate" Sheet on page 52. Then try to discuss these different attitudes and ideas. This won't be difficult if you remember to be clear about your answers. *Stay calm* even when you feel yourself getting heated up over an issue you don't care to discuss or an answer that's different from yours.

8. *You must compromise.* This means you may have to give in once in a while. If it isn't critical, why not?

9. *Your parents must compromise.* This means *they* may have to give in once in a while. If it isn't critical, why not?

10. Remember: Your parents honestly have your best interests at heart. It is a curse that children and, incidentally, their parents, must bear! Consider the valuable experience they have accumulated during their lives. If your parents are working with you on this guide, it's proof that they honestly want to help you.

11. When you have completed your listening and discussion meetings, list the factors that are most critical to your overall education in college. Use the Priorities for College Selection sheet we've included on page 53.

Completing these worksheets will help you establish your priorities for college selection and stay focused on the college selection process. Like any smart consumer, you have to know what you're shopping for before you can hope to find it.

In addition, these answers, coupled with the material in your record file (see chapter 6), will help you prepare a resume. Why bother to do all this now? Because it's ultimately *your* responsibility to find a college at which you'll be happy, comfortable, successful and able to study the subjects you want to study. This is a decision that can affect the rest of your life. It can't hurt to be prepared!

The Who Am I? Exercise

Please answer the following questions. For each question there may be more than one answer.

1. What are your best and strongest personality traits? (For example, are you *honest, warm and friendly, inquisitive, cheerful, motivated,* etc.?)

2. What are your best developed skills and abilities? (Are you *a good cook, a tennis buff, musician, athlete,* etc.?)

3. For each subject area listed below, check whether it's one in which you do best or worst, like best or least:

	DO BEST	LIKE BEST	DO WORST	LIKE LEAST
Art	☐	☐	☐	☐
Biology	☐	☒	☒	☐
Chemistry	☐	☒	☐	☐
Computers	☒	☐	☐	☐
English	☐	☐	☐	☒
Foreign Language	☒	☐	☐	☐
History	☒	☐	☐	☐
Math	☒	☐	☐	☐
Phys. Ed.	☒	☐	☐	☐
Physics	☐	☐	☐	☐
Psychology	☐	☐	☐	☐
Reading	☒	☐	☐	☐
Writing	☐	☐	☐	☐
Other subjects:				
____________________	☐	☐	☐	☐
____________________	☐	☐	☐	☐
____________________	☐	☐	☐	☐

School Activities

4. In which extracurricular activities have you been involved during high school? On the next page, check all that apply in the first box. Then rank your activities in order of their importance to you (with **1** being most important). Write the numbers in the second box.

ACTIVITY	INVOLVED IN	IMPORTANCE
Band	☐	☐
Baseball	☒	☒
Cable TV	☐	☐
Cheerleading	☐	☐
Cross Country	☐	☐
Danceline	☐	☐
Debate	☐	☐
Figure Skating	☐	☐
Football	☐	☐
Golf	☒	☒
Gymnastics	☐	☐
Hockey	☐	☐
Literary Magazine	☐	☐
Newspaper	☐	☐
Orchestra	☐	☐
Soccer	☐	☐
Speech/Declam	☐	☐
Student Government	☐	☐
Swimming	☐	☐
Tennis	☒	☒
Theater	☐	☐
Track	☐	☐
Wrestling	☐	☐
Yearbook	☐	☐

Other activities:

____________________	☐	☐
____________________	☐	☐
____________________	☐	☐

Activities Outside School

5. List any volunteer work you do.

6. List any private lessons you take or have taken during high school.

7. List any other clubs or organizations in which you are involved. Circle any that are particularly satisfying to you.

8. List any honors or awards you have received.

9. Are there any activities that you wish you had tried or would like to try? Please write them down.

10. Have you had any part-time or summer jobs that have made you curious to find out more about a particular field or profession? List those jobs.

Identifying Your Learning Style

The following series of questions will help you define how you learn best. This information is essential in your choosing a suitable college environment. Check the answer in each set that seems closest to your preference. If you have no particular preference in a particular set, leave the item blank.

11. While I am learning, I do best when I (or I prefer to):

A.
- ☒ Hear information
- ☐ See information

B.
- ☐ Look at diagrams
- ☒ Read descriptions in words

C.
- ☐ Look at maps
- ☒ Read directions

D.
- ☐ Write notes
- ☒ Concentrate on listening

E.
- ☒ Answer questions with definite "rights" or "wrongs"
- ☐ Answer questions that can be debated

F.
- ☒ Listen to music
- ☐ Have quiet
- ☐ Have TV on

G.
- ☒ Stretch out
- ☐ Sit in a chair

H.
- ☐ Study a little each day
- ☒ Study a lot of material all at once

I.
- ☐ Eat while I learn
- ☒ I don't need to eat while I learn

J.
- ☐ Am near a window
- ☐ Am away from the window

K.
- ☒ Have a lot of light (electric or sunlight)
- ☐ Have just enough so I can see

L.
- ☒ Study alone
- ☐ Study with a friend
- ☐ Study in a group

M.
- ☐ Have someone available for questions or help
- ☒ Study alone, but seek out help if needed

N.
- ☐ Study in the morning
- ☒ Study in the evening
- ☐ Study in the afternoon

O.
- ☒ Study under pressure
- ☐ Have ample time to study

P.
- ☐ Read a lot
- ☒ Read only what is required for classes

Q.
- ☒ Participate in doing something
- ☐ Be a spectator

12. How long can you concentrate well without a break?

- ☐ Less than 15 minutes
- ☒ 15-30 minutes
- ☐ 30 minutes-1 hour
- ☐ 1-2 hours
- ☐ More than 2 hours

13. How often do you feel bored in school?

- ❑ Never
- ❑ Infrequently
- ❑ Once a week
- ☒ At least once every day
- ❑ Most of every day
- ❑ All the time
- ❑ In certain classes (please list below)

14. Can you explain why you're bored at particular times or in certain classes?

15. What do you think you will need most in a college situation to be a successful learner? In other words, what environment best suits your learning style? Summarize the factors from this list that seem the most important to your learning. (And when you visit campuses, refer back to this list to determine if the college offers the kind of learning environment you need.)

16. What level of academic challenge do you want for yourself? Think about not only the *quality* of your education, but also about how much *stress and pressure* you think you

can handle and the *amount of time you want to pursue other interests and activities* outside of the college classroom. Check one of the choices below:

- ❑ The highest possible academic challenge
- ❑ A very strong academic challenge
- ☒ A very good school, but one that allows me to pursue other things
- ❑ A good school with a relaxed atmosphere

17. What career(s) or majors might interest you?

18. How far do you want to go in your career? Check one:

- ❑ To the top—highest income, highest prestige (remember: often the highest stress and effort).
- ❑ Do it well...make a good living, be successful and work hard!
- ❑ Be good at what I do, but have time and energy for other things.
- ❑ Make a living and enjoy life in other ways.

That completes your "Who Am I?" exercise. Review your answers carefully; make sure you've been truthful and accurate. Then go to chapter four to prepare for discussions with your parents and other planners. (The next chapter gives them the chance to answer the same questions about you.)

CHAPTER THREE

For Parents: Who Is Your Student?

In the previous chapter, we asked your student to answer a series of questions designed to help her learn more about herself, her likes and dislikes, strengths and weaknesses, plans and desires. Now it's *your* turn.

You've watched your child develop since birth. You know his or her favorite foods, tastes in clothes and music, maybe even the type of boyfriend or girlfriend he or she prefers. You have invested your time, money and energy (perhaps more of all three than you ever thought you would!) in this budding adult. You possess deep insights into that life. Your wisdom needs to be heard.

Because you as parents have invested so much of yourselves in your children, each of you probably has a somewhat different—and valuable—perspective about your child. And even without the exercises you and your student are performing as part of this book, you've certainly already discovered that your child has a perception of him- or herself that differs, perhaps sharply, from yours, your spouse's or anyone elses.

Each of you needs to be heard. Only then can sensible conclusions be reached.

How To Complete This Exercise

The Who Is Your Student? exercise in this chapter focuses on what we believe are the most critical factors in selecting colleges best suited for your child. (The Who Am I? exercise for the student in the previous chapter focuses on the same task.)

The rules for working on these exercises are designed to allow each person to contribute his or her own unique and valuable ideas. After each individual has been heard and understood, you can begin to negotiate. In the student section, we remind the student of how much wisdom and support you can offer him or her. By the same token, you should keep in mind that you are helping plan for the *student's* life!

At this point, you need to determine who will share in helping the student to know him- or herself and his or her educational needs better. We suggest both parents, if possible. Include others if you feel it will help the student. A note of caution: College planning involves considerable discussion of the student's life and the parents' finances. Include others only if <u>all of you</u> are willing to share these intimate details with them.

Because each person involved offers different insights, EACH PLANNER MUST COMPLETE THE WORKSHEET INDEPENDENTLY BEFORE ANY DISCUSSION OCCURS. So take a copy of this exercise into some quiet corner and write answers to the questions strictly on the basis of what *you alone* believe. (In the following chapter, which you and your student should read together, we'll explain how to set up and run a meeting to discuss your and his or her answers to these questions. And how that discussion or series of discussions will form the basis of the planning process to follow.)

The Who Is Your Student? Exercise

Please answer the following questions. For each question there may be more than one answer.

1. What are your student's best and strongest personality traits? (For example, is he or she *honest, warm and friendly, inquisitive, cheerful, motivated,* etc.?)

2. What are your student's best developed skills and abilities? (Is he or she *a good cook, a tennis buff, musician, athlete,* etc.?)

3. For each subject area listed below (and on the following page), check whether you think it's one in which your student does best or worst, likes best or least:

	DOES BEST	LIKES BEST	DOES WORST	LIKES LEAST
Art	❑	❑	❑	❑
Biology	❑	❑	❑	❑
Chemistry	❑	❑	❑	❑
Computers	❑	❑	❑	❑
English	❑	❑	❑	❑
Foreign Language	❑	❑	❑	❑
History	❑	❑	❑	❑
Math	❑	❑	❑	❑
Phys. Ed.	❑	❑	❑	❑

Physics	❑	❑	❑	❑
Psychology	❑	❑	❑	❑
Reading	❑	❑	❑	❑
Writing	❑	❑	❑	❑
Other subjects:				
________________	❑	❑	❑	❑
________________	❑	❑	❑	❑
________________	❑	❑	❑	❑

School Activities

4. In which extracurricular activities has your student been involved during high school? Check all that apply in the first box. Then rank these activities in the order that reflects how beneficial you believe each is to your student (with **1** being most important). Write the numbers in the second box.

ACTIVITY	INVOLVED IN	IMPORTANCE
Band	❑	❑
Baseball	❑	❑
Cable TV	❑	❑
Cheerleading	❑	❑
Cross Country	❑	❑
Danceline	❑	❑
Debate	❑	❑
Figure Skating	❑	❑
Football	❑	❑
Golf	❑	❑
Gymnastics	❑	❑
Hockey	❑	❑
Literary Magazine	❑	❑
Newspaper	❑	❑

Orchestra	❑	❑
Soccer	❑	❑
Speech/Declam	❑	❑
Student Government	❑	❑
Swimming	❑	❑
Tennis	❑	❑
Theater	❑	❑
Track	❑	❑
Wrestling	❑	❑
Yearbook	❑	❑
Other activities:		
____________	❑	❑
____________	❑	❑
____________	❑	❑

Activities Outside School

5. List any volunteer work the student does.

6. List any private lessons the student takes or has taken during high school.

7. List any other clubs or organizations in which the student is involved. Circle any that you think are particularly satisfying to him or her.

8. List any honors or awards the student has received.

9. Are there any activities that you wish the student had tried or would like him or her to try? Please write them down.

10. Has the student had any part-time or summer jobs that made him or her curious to find out more about a particular field or profession? List those jobs.

The following series of questions will help you think about how the student learns best. This information is essential in your student's choice of a suitable college environment. Check the answer in each set that seems closest to your preference.

As a parent, you may not be aware of the answers to many of these learning styles questions. However, sharing your perceptions here will definitely help your student. So will listening carefully (and respectfully) to your student's responses to this section.

Please answer any of the sections that you have even a hunch about. Leave those to which you honestly have no answer blank.

11. While the student is learning, he or she does best when he or she:

A. ❑ Hears information
❑ Sees information

B. ❑ Looks at diagrams
❑ Reads descriptions in words

C. ❑ Looks at maps
❑ Reads directions

D. ❑ Writes notes
❑ Concentrates on listening

E. ❑ Answers questions with definite "rights" or "wrongs"
❑ Answers questions that can be debated

F. ❑ Listens to music
❑ Has quiet
❑ Has TV on

G. ❑ Stretches out
❑ Sits in a chair
❑ Sits at a table or desk

H. ❑ Studies a little each day
❑ Studies a lot of material all at once

I. ❑ Eats while he or she learns
❑ Doesn't need to eat while he or she learns

J. ❑ Is near a window
❑ Is away from the window

K. ❑ Has a lot of light (electric or sunlight)
❑ Has just enough to see

L. ❑ Studies alone
❑ Studies with a friend
❑ Studies in a group

M. ❑ Has someone available for questions or help
❑ Studies on his or her own, but seeks out help if he or she really needs it

N. ❑ Studies in the morning
❑ Studies in the evening
❑ Studies in the afternoon

O. ❑ Studies under pressure
❑ Allows ample time to study

P. ❑ Reads a lot
❑ Reads only what is required for classes

Q. ❑ Participates in doing something
❑ Prefers to watch and observe

12. How long can your student concentrate well without a break?

❑ Less than 15 minutes
❑ 15-30 minutes
❑ 30 minutes-1 hour
❑ 1-2 hours
❑ More than 2 hours

13. How often does your student feel bored in school?

❑ Never
❑ Infrequently
❑ Once a week
❑ At least once every day
❑ Most of every day
❑ All the time
❑ In certain classes (please list on next page)

Classes in which the student is bored:

14. Can you explain why he or she is bored at particular times or in certain classes?

15. What do you think the student needs most in a college situation to be a successful learner?

16. What level of academic challenge do you think would most benefit your student? Please consider not only the *quality* of education, but also about how much *stress and pressure* you think the student can handle and the student's ability to make time for other interests and needs beyond strictly academic requirements. Check one of the choices below:

- ❑ The highest possible academic challenge
- ❑ A very strong academic challenge
- ❑ A very good school, but one that allows the student time to pursue other things
- ❑ A good school with a relaxed atmosphere

17. What career(s) or majors interest your student?

18. How far do you honestly want your student to go in his or her career? Check one:

- ❑ To the top—highest income, highest prestige (remember: often the highest stress and effort)
- ❑ Do it well...make a good living, be successful and work hard
- ❑ Be good at what he or she does, but have time and energy for other things
- ❑ Make a living and enjoy life in other ways

That completes your "Who Is Your Student?" exercise. Review your answers carefully; make sure you've been truthful and accurate. Then go to the next chapter to prepare for discussions with your student and other planners.

CHAPTER FOUR

For All Planners: Sharing Your Differences

The next step after everyone completes the appropriate worksheets from the two previous chapters is to schedule a listening meeting among your family's college planners.

As the name implies, everyone attends to *hear and understand* how others responded to the "Who Are I?/Who Is Your Student?" exercises, not to get on a soapbox, argue or dictate. Allow about one hour for the meeting. This may be sufficient for some families to complete all their discussion.

It may well *not* be enough time (and don't read anything negative into the fact that it wasn't enough for *your* family!). You may even have to schedule a *series* of meetings to give everyone a chance to talk, discuss and respond to all the points that need to be brought out. Allow as much time as *your* family needs, no matter *how* much time that is. Remember, the time you make available now from your hectic schedule and the information and communication that surface will save you loads of money and heartache later.

Rules For Successful Meetings

First, set up a definite time for your meeting with the family's college planners to discuss everyone's answers to the worksheets. This meeting should take priority over dates, working late, extracurricular activities, phone calls, etc. It should be considered the *top* priority for your whole family.

As a direct result of the many planning workshops we've led with a variety of families, we have developed a set of rules for the listening meeting that have worked for us. If everyone agrees to observe these rules, we guarantee *you* will have a successful meeting, too:

1. Select one person at a time to share responses.

2. ONLY THAT PERSON PROVIDES INFORMATION, FEELINGS, IDEAS.

3. Other planners listen thoughtfully.

4. Listeners MAY NOT SPEAK OR RESPOND ALOUD until the speaker is finished. Jot down your responses and save them for the negotiating time. Suppress the urge to blurt out something like "you're dreaming!" And don't claim you're following the rules just because you've bitten your tongue—try not to reflect judgement by body positions, facial expressions, sighs or other non-verbal cues. You are there to try to *understand* what the other people are saying, not to agree, disagree or argue your own point-of-view. You'll have your own turn to share your responses in a few minutes and a chance to debate others' responses later.

5. When a speaker has finished discussing an item, listeners may ask clarifying questions to be sure that they under-

stand what they've heard or to gain additional information *from the speaker*, not from each other. Some examples: "Did I understand you to say that you believe you're equally good at English and math?" or "Would I be correct to say that you feel that you enjoy football the most, but your music might benefit you more?" Give the speaker time to confirm your clarification or to restate his or her position. "Why?" is an acceptable question under virtually all circumstances. Stating why you believe something is inaccurate is *not* acceptable at any time, nor is sharing your own experience when you are a listener, such as "Well, son, when I was in school..."

The Listening Meeting

Decide who speaks first. If no one's particularly concerned about order, allow the student to share his or her responses to questions 1-4 on the Who Am I? sheet, followed by other planners' answers to the same questions on their worksheets. Continue in the same fashion with questions 5-10, then 11-18.

During the meeting, the student should take notes on every answer or part of an answer on which all planners agree. Use the **"We Agree"** sheet at the end of this chapter to summarize these notes. One of the other planners should volunteer to take notes on the answers or parts of answers on which the planners disagree. These should then be summarized on the **"Up for Debate"** list, also at the end of this chapter. Remember: These notes are taken and summaries written prior to any discussion of everyone's answers; indeed, they will act as the basis for that discussion.

The Discussing Meeting

Once all planners have had a chance to give their responses to all the questions, you need to discuss each of your reactions to what you have heard. This can be done at the same session as the listening meeting—if (and *only* if) *all* of you have enough time and patience—or you can schedule another meeting or series of meetings to continue the discussion. The amount of time or number of meetings you schedule will, of course, depend on the number of issues you know need to be discussed. If you have no idea how long it will take, allow one hour and see how it goes.

Begin your discussion by reading aloud the list of "We Agree" items. Make certain that you all actually *do* agree before you move on! Your list might read: "We agree that John is best in math and also likes that subject the best. John needs to be alone a lot when he studies. He wants to play soccer in college." Sound simple? It is!

Now on to the stickier issues—those matters on which you disagree. Example: John wants to attend a college in Florida so he can play baseball year-round (one with a reputation for "sun and fun"); Dad wants him to attend his Midwest alma mater and concentrate more on his studies; Mom is neutral. Remember: There are no right or wrong answers here, even if the emotions that may surface cloak themselves in judgmental language ("No son of mine is going to go to some Miami party school!") *Expect disagreements*. We can't remember a family who did all the exercises in this book and agreed on *everything!* Work toward understanding each other, then try to decide what is best for *the student.*

Try the listening and understanding strategy first: Why does each person feel as they do? Planners may state arguments to overcome others' objections, but remember: "Stating an argument" doesn't mean shouting out a nonnegotiable demand or dictating behavior. Take your time, be patient and don't get angry. If no solution or resolution to a particular disagreement can be reached in fifteen minutes, table that topic and schedule it for a second meeting. Continue to list topics for further consideration on the Up for Debate sheet. (Be sure to schedule the second meeting before concluding this one.)

No matter how far apart you seem to be on a particular question, continue to search for compromises. In the above example, the family agreed that John would consider applying to other "warm weather" schools that offered the higher academic standards Dad wants and the year-round sunshine John wants. Dad agrees John can continue to play baseball as long as his grades stay above average. And John agrees that his studies should be a higher priority.

When you have completed your listening and discussion meetings, list the factors that are most critical to the student's overall education. (Use the **"Priorities for College Selection"** page that follows.)

You're starting to get organized and focused! Good work!

WE AGREE

UP FOR DEBATE

PRIORITIES FOR COLLEGE SELECTION

CHAPTER FIVE

Exploring Careers

STUDENT

The object of career exploration is to pinpoint possibilities and rule out inappropriate options. It *does not* mean that you must decide what you are going to do for the rest of your life... right now! Whether or not you have the faintest clue about the career you will eventually pursue, you *should* begin thinking about possible career choices. Obviously, any decisions you make now will affect the major you hope to pursue in college (and, most probably, the choice of the college).

It's perfectly understandable if you're really uncertain at this point. But it's important to at least be aware of the many academic options available to you when you are shopping for colleges. For example: You're a whiz in math and assume you will become an engineer. Given your good grades, attending a highly competitive technological college like MIT or Cal Tech seems logical.

But what if you're not just a science whiz, but very talented in writing, too? Would the same hi-tech colleges give you the opportunity to develop your writing talents? And what will happen if you decide after your freshman or sophomore year to forego science and pursue a writing or editing career instead.

In a "high-tech" school, you may not even have the option of a writing major; even if you do, you may find yourself outside the mainstream of that school's science-oriented students. And it's rare to find a school that's at the top of the science pyramid but equally well-known for its writing program.

Why not think about attending a school that offers a solid program in your intended major, but equally solid programs in other subjects of interest to you? In other words, be flexible in planning for your education (otherwise known as *keeping your options open).*

If you're lucky enough to be blessed with a variety of abilities and talents, career exploration is significantly *more* important, not less so. You already *know* you can be successful in a wide range of fields or careers. While identifying those careers that will utilize many of your talents and maximize your abilities may seem easier for you, you still need to identify those that will mesh with your values, lifestyle and personal preferences. Considering and weighing these factors takes considerably more work than simply choosing a career on the basis of the starting salary and prestige.

Start by using the "Who Am I?" sheets to determine your already-established academic and extracurricular priorities. Then take this exercise one step further and ask yourself, "What is it about the subjects and activities I like that excites me?" For example, if you've established you love chemistry, try to discover just what about it fascinates you. Do you like seeing the results of chemical reactions for the sake of the changes? Do you enjoy creating something? Do you like to tackle new problems? Or do you want to understand the universe at a basic level? The answers to these questions will reveal even more about yourself and what you enjoy doing.

Next, you should thoughtfully examine your values and those of your parents. Complete the Value Pac Exercise on the following pages. Will the careers you are examining allow you to live by your values? Ask your parents if their work meshes or conflicts with *their* personal values.

This is also an ideal time to explore the potential life styles that future careers offer. Consider not only your values, but your and your parents' current standard of living. What kind of requirements will you have as a college graduate for material items like housing and transportation? What plans do you have for marriage and/or children? How much time do you want to spend in completing your education? After graduation, how much time do you want devote to work? How much to leisure?

The Value Pac exercise below will help you and your parents clarify your values and find where they match.

The Value Pac Exercise

Definitions Of Values

MORALITY
The belief in and keeping of ethical standards.

CREATIVE
The creating of new and innovative ideas and designs.

EMOTIONAL WELL-BEING
Freedom from overwhelming anxieties and barriers to effective functioning; peace of mind; inner security.

LOVE
Affection based on admiration or benevolence; warm attachment, enthusiasm or devotion; unselfish devotion that freely accepts another in loyalty and seeks his/her good.

RELIGION
Communion with, obedience to an activity on behalf of a supreme being.

KNOWLEDGE
The seeing of truth, information or principles for the satisfaction of curiosity, for use or for the power of knowing.

PHYSICAL APPEARANCE
Concern for the beauty of one's own body.

HONESTY
Fairness or straightforwardness of conduct; integrity; uprightness of character or action.

WEALTH
Abundance of valuable possessions or resources; affluence.

HEALTH
The condition of being sound in body; freedom from physical disease or pain; the general condition of the body; well-being.

ACHIEVEMENT
Accomplishment; a result brought about by resolve, persistence or endeavor. The word "achieve" is defined as "to bring to a successful conclusion, accomplishment."

LOYALTY
Maintaining allegiance to a person, group, institution or political entity.

PLEASURE
The agreeable emotion accompanying the possession or expectation of what is good or greatly desired, "pleasure" stresses satisfaction rather than visible happiness.

AUTONOMY
The ability to be a self-determining individual.

POWER
Possession of control, authority, or influence over others.

ALTRUISM
Regard for or devotion to the interests of others.

RECOGNITION
Being made to feel significant and important; being given special notice or attention.

WISDOM
The ability to discern inner qualities and relationships; insight, good sense, judgement.

SKILL
The ability to use one's knowledge effectively and readily in execution or performance; technical expertise.

JUSTICE
The quality of being impartial or fair; righteousness; conformity to truth, fact or reason; to treat others fairly or adequately.

AESTHETIC
The appreciation and enjoyment of beauty for beauty's sake.

Use these explanations to answer the questions below:

1. Identify your top five values from those listed in the 'Value Pac" and explain why they are important to you.

2. Identify your bottom five values and explain why they are not as important to you.

3. Have one or both parent identify their top five and bottom five values and explain their reasons for each position.

4. Describe one value you have picked up from your parent(s) and explain how this has occurred.

5. As you discuss this with your parent(s), describe any new insights you gain in the process.

(Activity reprinted from *Proactive Counseling*. St. Paul, MN: Minnesota Department of Education, 1986. By permission of its author, Joel Anderson.)

Planning Your Future

Keep in mind that you need to remain flexible and open to the demands of the future in your career development. You must realize the potential for personal impact of economic and leadership changes in all business environments, including high technology, health care, education and industry. Many good books are available that describe jobs, current starting salaries, educational requirements and future prospects in many fields. (See the Resource List in chapter 14.)

Informational Interviews

After you have identified a few possible career options, **informational interviews** can provide a valuable way to obtain first-hand knowledge about those careers. From your list of career possibilities, try to arrange visits with professionals already working in those fields. Don't be afraid—people love to talk about their work and can be delightfully supportive of a young person. People employed within a particular field can give you practical insights into their daily work activities, career paths and how they mesh the requirements of their careers with their personal value systems. You should be able to extract enough ideas from these interviews to determine if you really wish to continue your pursuit of a specific career.

Locate potential candidates through your parents, friends, teachers, association directories (available at the local library), the phone book or other imaginative tactics. Be willing to take a chance and perhaps suffer the disappointment of a "no." (If that happens on your first try, don't give up. Ask that person if he or she has a friend or colleague in the same field who would be interested in giving you an informational interview.)

Try to arrange the meeting at the person's office or work site. Be prepared with a good list of questions about how that person started in the field, his or her educational background, current job duties and how the job fits into his or her personal lifestyle. (See sample questions in the next section for help.)

Do your homework before you go on the interview. Find out about the company, its services and products, and as much as you can about the person you are going to interview. Is he or she well-known in the field? Has he or she had any outstanding achievements? The business section of the local library can help you locate information on local companies. Alternatively, you may call the company directly and request informational and promotional brochures.

This process may be a little uncomfortable at first. If you want some additional advice on how to go about it, ask your parents or your school guidance counselor. But no matter how uncomfortable such interviews make you, try them. They are an excellent chance for you to learn how to develop your own opportunities, a *learned* skill that will be most useful for the rest of your life. After all, almost every job you get in your life will probably come about because of your own ***networking***—using your acquaintances and colleagues as valuable sources of leads, contacts and other information.

PARENTS

You may feel as uncomfortable with the informational interview as your student. It's a good time to talk with your student about similar experiences from your own life—your first job interview, for example. Encourage the student to develop his or her opportunities and not to be discouraged when something doesn't go exactly as planned.

STUDENT

Here are some sample questions to use on your informational interview:

1. How did you become interested in this field?

2. Where did you go to school? What was your major? How long did it take you to prepare for an entry-level job?

3. Other than education, what other personal traits does a person need to be successful in your field?

4. What other experiences did you have that helped you get started in this career?

5. How did you get to your current position?

6. What do you do on a daily basis? (Note: Be sure you ask enough exploratory questions to get a detailed answer.)

7. What do you particularly like about your daily work?

8. What do you like least about your daily work?

9. What future do you see for this kind of work? Would you encourage me to consider this line of work as a career?

10. What kind of lifestyle does this career allow? How many hours must you work weekly?

11. Other than income, how does this career benefit you and your family?

12. What colleges are known for providing good preparation in your field?

13. What can I major in to help me prepare for a career similar to yours?

14. What advice can you give me as I consider this field and begin my college search and education?

On-the-Job Experience

An excellent way to explore potential careers is to actually get a job in that field. There are a number of possible ways to accomplish this:

1. **Mentorship programs:** A student is teamed with a professional in his or her field of interest. The student develops a one-to-one relationship with the mentor and first-hand experience in a particular field. (Non-paid)

2. **Internships:** A student is placed with a company or organization in his or her field of interest, either part-time during the school year or full-time during the summer. Generally, the company is asked to evaluate the student's work or progress, and the student receives a grade and/or credits at the end of the internship. (Sometimes offer minimal pay; more often non-paid experience.)

3. **Work/study programs:** A student becomes a paid employee of a company or organization, generally working a set number of hours at or near minimum wage.

4. **Volunteering:** The student can set up a volunteer experience through a local church or community service organization to gain valuable experience in a field of interest. (Obviously, non-paid.)

5. **Paid jobs:** Part-time work while the student is still in high school provides more than just spending money. The student will gain valuable experience and the chance to prove that he or she is ready to take on ever-increasing responsibilities. If the student is planning to pay his or her own way through college—or to contribute to the parents' payments —now is also a good time to start working and saving.

Naturally, if you're going to work, try to get a job in the field that interests you. If you love animals, maybe a job at "burger heaven" is not your best bet; try for an entry-level job with a veterinarian.

If you find you don't like what you have experienced, that's wonderful! Your high school years afford you the luxury of ruling out options and trying new ones. And let you gain more experience and knowledge in the process.

CHAPTER SIX

Keeping Records & Preparing Resumes

BOTH

The reason for organizing records is to be more efficient and accurate when completing college and financial aid applications; in responding to specific inquiries from college admissions offices, testing companies and scholarship sources; and in resume writing.

Records do NOT belong scattered throughout the household or dumped into the family "record file" in a kitchen drawer. Organizing the student's records in a single location, filed by topic, will save the whole family time, energy and stress.

So start by deciding upon a single location in which to store the student's personal records. Develop a good filing system that will not only organize papers, but also teach the student valuable organizational skills. If you don't own a file cabinet, consider buying one of two products available at most stationery or office supply stores: an expandable pocket portfolio or a solid plastic file box (sturdier, but less compact). In either container, designate a separate folder for each of the following categories of the student's important documents:

What You Should Save

• REPORT CARDS

Along with actual report cards, you might save samples of the student's work—especially in high school. The actual work easily records interests, talents, difficulties and accomplishments. Work samples will also come in handy when you request letters of recommendation from past employers.

• TRANSCRIPTS/GPA/CLASS RANK

Transcripts are the high school's official record of the student's academic history from grades 9 - 12. They are generally kept in the guidance office. Make sure honors courses are noted in the transcript.

The GPA (Grade Point Average) is usually found on the transcript. High schools generally calculate this by computing credits times a numerical grade equivalent (often "A" = 4.0, "B" = 3.0, etc.). Class rank is simply a listing of GPAs, from highest to lowest. Example: 75/306 (75th out of a class of 306 students).

• STANDARDIZED TEST SCORES

Be sure the student understands them. Read the test booklet, then ask a teacher or counselor to explain anything you don't understand.

• ACTIVITY RECORDS

From elementary, junior high and high school. This should be a comprehensive list of sports, music and other extracurricular or special activities in which the student has participated either inside or outside school.

• **AWARDS/HONORS**

List award name, date received and significance of the award. Example: Peabody Scholar, 1987, awarded to Jefferson High School senior who demonstrates musical prowess and an interest in pursuing a musical career.

• **WORK/VOLUNTEER RECORDS**

List each job title, dates of employment, business address, responsibilities. Any work experience, from babysitting to lawn mowing, should be listed. Also list any volunteer work, even if it was only for one day.

• **MEDICAL RECORDS**

Include immunization records and health and disease history from birth until the present.

• **INSURANCE RECORDS**

Check to see if the family policies cover the student when he or she is at school. If so, call the insurance company and order a card for the student.

• **FINANCIAL RECORDS**

Include information about the student's financial status: savings and checking accounts, tax returns, stocks or other student-owned holdings.

You will need these when you begin financial planning for college.

• **TRAVEL RECORDS**

Keep a list of the student's travel experiences and, perhaps, some personal reactions to each trip. Travel experience helps demonstrate that the student is well-rounded, and the written reactions might prompt responses to college application essay questions.

STUDENT

THIS IS NOT THE TIME OR PLACE TO BE MODEST! Keep track of all your accomplishments, no matter how trivial they may seem to you. Not only will this information help you plan for college, but it's fun to remember what you've done. Brainstorm about what you've gained from your experiences and be sure you are able to talk about what you've accomplished. You probably have more to offer than you think!

From this growing collection of records and achievements, you will begin to get a clearer picture of what you really have to offer the world.

Creating Your First Resume

Your resume is a one- or two-page summary of you—your education, skills, employment experience and academic/career objective(s). It is not a biography, but a "quick and clean" way to identify and describe you to college recruiters and admissions officers.

Your resume can also be an excellent organizational tool, putting the data you'll need for filling out college applications at your fingertips. You can also include your resume with each college and scholarship application packet.

In order to begin preparing your resume, you will need to assemble all the following information (which should have been done in the previous section. If not, go back and try again!):

1. The name and address of your high school; expected graduation date.

2. Your grade point average and class rank. (Express the latter as the number of completed trimester or semester grades your rank includes. For example: 100/308, includes six semesters, freshman through junior year.)

3. Important classes you've taken, especially those that relate to your intended college major.

4. A concise academic/career objective.

5. Clubs, honor societies and other extracurricular activities—name of each and dates in which you participated. This can include high school, junior high school, even elementary school activities. (Be sure you include any leadership positions you held.)

6. Awards and honors you have received.

7. The names, addresses and telephone numbers of all your past employers.

8. The key personnel with whom you worked and a concise summary of the work you performed.

9. Any letters of recommendation from these employers, your teachers, counselors, etc.

10. Hobbies and other interests.

11. A list of references.

12. If you went into the military from high school and are now applying to college, you should also collect pertinent service records.

Once you have this information in hand, you have a lot of options about what to include or leave out. In general, we suggest you always include the following data:

1. Your name, address and telephone number.

2. Pertinent educational history (including grades, class rank, activities, etc.)

3. Pertinent work history

4. Academic honors

5. Memberships in organizations.

You have the option of including the following:

1. Your academic/career objective
2. Personal data
3. Hobbies
4. Military service history (if applicable)
5. References

And you should *never* include the following:

1. Photographs or illustrations (of yourself or anything else!).

Guidelines For Resume Preparation

Your resume should be limited to a single page if possible, two at most. When you're laying out the resume, try to leave a reasonable amount of "white space"—generous margins all around and spacing between entries.

Be brief. Use phraseology rather than complete sentences. Your resume is a summary of your talents, not an English Lit paper. Choose your words carefully and use "power words" whenever possible. "Organized" is more powerful than "put together;" "supervised" better than "oversaw;" "formulated" better than "thought up." Strong words like these can make the most mundane clerical work sound like a series of responsible, professional positions. And, of course, they will tend to make your resume stand out. Here's a "starter list" of words which you may want to use in your resume:

achieved	administered	advised
analyzed	applied	arranged
budgeted	calculated	classified
communicated	completed	computed
conceptualized	coordinated	critiqued
delegated	determined	developed
devised	directed	established

evaluated	executed	formulated
gathered	generated	guided
implemented	improved	initiated
instituted	instructed	introduced
invented	issued	launched
lectured	litigated	lobbied
managed	negotiated	operated
organized	overhauled	planned
prepared	presented	presided
programmed	promoted	recommended
researched	reviewed	revised
reorganized	regulated	selected
solved	scheduled	supervised
systematized	taught	tested
traced	trained	updated
utilized	wrote	

An important suggestion: When you've completed writing and designing your resume, have a couple of close friends or family members proofread it for typographical errors *before* you type it or send it to the printer. For some reason, the more you check it yourself, the less likely you'll catch the errors you missed the first time around. A fresh look from someone not as familiar with it will catch these glaring (and potentially embarrassing) errors before they're duplicated a couple of hundred times.

It should be typed or printed (not xeroxed) on 8 1/2" x 11" white, cream or ivory stock. (Note: Printing does *not* mean typesetting; a cleanly-typed resume is certainly more than acceptable.) The ink should be black or, at most, a royal blue. Don't scrimp on the paper quality—use the best bond you can afford. And since printing 100 or even 200 copies will cost little more than 50, if you do decide to print your resume, *over*estimate your needs, and opt for the highest quantity you think you may need. Prices at various "quick print" storefronts will not break the bank; but the quality look printing affords may leave the right impression.

When you request letters of recommendation from teachers, counselors, coaches or friends, give them a copy of your resume with the recommendation form. Not only will that make their task easier, but you'll probably get a clearer and more detailed recommendation from them. For example, your English 12 teacher may have forgotten about your role in a musical during your sophomore year. When he sees your resume, he'll recall the insights from the experience that you have shared in class. In your recommendation, he can comment on how you are currently applying those insights in English 12.

We have prepared a fill-in-the-blanks resume form on the following pages that will allow you to create an effective resume within minutes. This is no time to be humble! List everything you've done, even if it seems trivial to you. It's also not the time to exaggerate! Be truthful!

FILL-IN-THE-BLANKS RESUME OUTLINE

Name: ______________________________

Address: ______________________________

City, state, zip code: ______________________________

Telephone number: ______________________________

• OBJECTIVE (Example: To be accepted to a liberal arts college in the upper Midwest offering a superior English literature major program.):

____

____

• EDUCATION:

High school name: ______________________________

High school address: ______________________________

Expected graduation date: ______________________________

Grade point average: ______________ Class rank: ______________

Important classes you have taken, especially if they relate to your intended major in college:

____

____

____

• EXTRACURRICULAR ACTIVITIES (Activity name and dates participated):

____

____

____

____

____

• AWARDS AND HONORS (Award name, date received and the significance of the award. Example: Wilson Pickering Scholarship, 1987, awarded to senior student at Peabody High School with superior academic achievements and an expressed interest in pursuing higher education in the natural sciences.):

____

____

____

• WORK EXPERIENCE (Job title, name of business, business address, dates of employment and your major responsibilities. Include volunteer experience in this category. List your experiences with the *most recent dates first!):*

____

____

____

____

____

____

____

____

____

____

• INTERESTS AND HOBBIES:

____

____

____

____

____

• REFERENCES (A list of at least three names with their titles, addresses and telephone numbers. Before you include anyone on this list, talk with them and make sure you have their permission to use their name as a reference. You should also ask them what they are willing to say about you to a potential school, program or employer. You may want to list the same people from whom you request letters of recommendation.):

1. ____

____

____

2. ____

____

____

3. ____

____

____

4. ____

____

____

5. ____

____

____

SAMPLE COMPLETED RESUME

GILDA H. TURNER
80 Stemmons Freeway,
Dallas, TX 87540
(214)788-0000

OBJECTIVE

To be accepted to a Midwest liberal arts college offering a superior program in English literature.

EDUCATION

Graduating in June, 1988, from Dethis High School (421 Fifth St., Dallas, TX 87541. 214-788-0489). College prep core curriculum including honors English 11 and 12.

GPA 3.2 (A=4.0); Class rank: 78/352.

EXTRACURRICULAR ACTIVITIES

Writers Club (President—1986 & 1987); Yearbook staff (Editor—1987-88); Field hockey (4 years); Cheer squad (3 years); United Way.

HONORS & AWARDS

National Honor Society. Senior Class President.

WORK EXPERIENCE

1985 & 1986 (summers) Kisch Publishing Co., 842 Dallas Pike, Dallas, TX 87440. Intern in editorial department. Duties included reading manuscripts, typing editor's reports, filing.

1986 & 1987 (school year) Simmons Public Library (831 5th Ave., Simmons, TX 87550). Library assistant. Duties included cataloguing, typing and filing.

INTERESTS & HOBBIES

Reading, writing, sports

REFERENCES

Available upon request

CHAPTER SEVEN

Taking The Tests

STUDENT

Most four-year colleges require that you take some sort of standardized test (college entrance exams), usually during your junior or senior years of high school. There are a variety of different tests, and each college to which you apply may well require a different combination of them. Be certain to check carefully which tests each college on your Shopping List requires (see next chapter).

These standardized tests are administered to quantify your skills, abilities and potential for success in college. For the most part, they concentrate on measuring your verbal and math skills.

As important as such tests are, remember: They are only one part of your "candidate profile" for any given college. People may succeed in college even if they score poorly on the entrance tests. Recently some colleges have eliminated entrance exam requirements—these institutions feel that one day's test production might not fairly represent a high school student's performance or ability level.

You will register for these tests in your high school guidance office.

A Variety Of Entrance Tests

ACT [American College Test]

Most commonly administered in the Midwestern United States. For further information, write to: ACT Registration, P.O. Box 414, Iowa City, Iowa 52243. Students with special needs should call 319-337-1332.

SAT [Scholastic Aptitude Test]

The major entrance test, offered nationwide. You'll receive two proficiency scores, one for verbal skills (V), one for math (M).

Register for the SAT in your high school guidance office. Make sure you pick up a Registration Bulletin at that time—it will answer any questions you may have regarding the test and where to get further information, should you need it.

This bulletin also contains a coupon for an Index of Majors book that may be ordered and paid for at registration time. This book identifies majors and the colleges that offer them; it's a valuable tool if purchased early enough in your college search. Your high school guidance office should also have this book.

The first registration deadline for the SAT will be in September; there are various test dates throughout the school year. You *must* coordinate your test taking dates with your chosen colleges' application deadlines—there's nothing worse than discovering an application deadline has passed before the next test date rolls around.

Your test scores will automatically be sent to the schools you specify on your SAT registration form. If you choose to take the SAT more than once, colleges *will* see *all* of your test scores, not just the latest ones.

AT [Achievement Tests]

Required by 150 of the most competitive colleges. ATs fall into five general categories: English, history, mathematics, foreign languages and science. There are several different tests in each category. Different colleges require different sets of ATs. Be sure to check which ATs each college requires and *by what date*.

Avoid a repeat of the sad tale of a young woman who didn't bother to check which tests her top college choice required. She took three ATs, only to discover her prospective college required the chemistry AT, not the biology AT she had taken. The next test date for the chemistry AT fell after the application deadline; her incomplete application to that school was disqualified.

The Registration Bulletin for the ATs is available in your guidance counselor's office. Note the registration deadlines and test-taking dates and mark them on your Planning Calendar (see chapter 12).

If certain ATs are required, you will need to more carefully plan your own testing schedule. NOTE: The SAT and the ATs <u>cannot be taken on the same day</u>. Coordinate the actual test dates with the date that the college admissions office requires they be received. Allow enough time for the testing service to score your test and send the results to the college (usually five to ten weeks).

The SAT and ATs are both administered by The College Board Admissions Testing Program (ATP). For general information, write: College Board ATP, CN 6200, Princeton, New Jersey 08541- 6200. Those of you on the East Coast should call the Princeton office — (609) 771-7600. Those on the West Coast should phone the California number — (415) 849-0950. Office hours are listed in the registration guide.

IMPORTANT NOTE: The Princeton telephone number is almost impossible to reach on the day before a test date. So plan ahead and avoid an emergency situation where a telephone call may be necessary at such a time.

PSAT [Preliminary Scholarship Aptitude Test]

A shorter, "practice" version of the SAT given in October of your junior year (though in some cases, you may take the PSAT in the ninth or tenth grade). The PSAT is administered by high schools. NOTE: If you took the PSAT before your junior year, you must retake it in the eleventh grade to qualify for National Merit Scholarships.

Register for this test several weeks in advance through your high school guidance office or the College Testing Board's Educational Service in Princeton, N.J. Address any correspondence to PSAT to the same address listed under the SAT section. The PSAT telephone numbers for special needs or questions: East Coast — (215) 750-8300 (call before 4 pm EST); West Coast — (415) 849-0950.

Registration Tips

Know well in advance the dates the tests you need are offered. Plan to take the tests well before the earliest of your college admissions deadlines, so all colleges will receive the results on time. You can take your SAT or ACT early enough so that you have time to take them again if your scores are lower than you'd hoped or expected. As we noted above, you can request to have results sent directly to the colleges where you are applying when you register for the tests. Many schools do prefer to receive test results directly from the testing service.

It might be wise to check the family social calendar and note weddings, graduations or trips that may conflict with proposed test dates. Consider any future athletic event, recital performance or anything else that may require your presence and possibly (or even remotely) conflict with a test date. The tests are pressure enough—you don't need any more!

Preparing For The Tests

If you wish to prepare for these tests in advance, there are several resources available to assist you:

1. The Resource List (chapter 14) recommends a number of books you may find helpful.

2. When you register for the SAT, your guidance counselor may give you a free copy of "Taking the SAT." This booklet will give you directions, sample questions and help you prepare for the test. We've found it helpful.

3. Your high school may offer a testing preparatory course. And your school district may offer a test preparation class after school or on a weekend through its community education program.

4. You may study at home with computer software preparations guides. Check with the guidance office first—your high school may have already purchased such software for students' use.

5. If you feel that you are weak in specific subject areas that are included in the tests, you or your parents can hire a tutor to help you. If you want to hire a tutor, start your search with the guidance office, principal, a teacher, or even a friend who may have had a tutoring experience. If you do decide to hire a tutor, work on topics that offer long-range benefits, not just improve your test scores.

6. There may be private educational companies in your community that offer test preparatory courses. Their names can be found in your local telephone directory's commercial (Yellow) pages under "educational consultants."

7. Finally, there are national educational companies that offer test preparation courses and other educational service programs. The three best known, each of which offers such

TEST PREPARATION SERVICES WORKSHEET

	COMPANY 1	COMPANY 2	COMPANY 3
Name			
Address			
Telephone			
Contact			
Services: For students For parents			
Staff Qualifications			

TEST PREPARATION SERVICES WORKSHEET (Continued)

	COMPANY 1	COMPANY 2	COMPANY 3
Fees			
Long-term value?			
Other benefits?			
Brochure available?			
Date brochure requested			

services in many locations nationwide, are listed below, along with their toll-free telephone numbers:

1. Huntington Learning Center — 800-692-8400

2. The Princeton Review — 800-525-6447

3. Stanley Kaplan — 800-KAP-TEST

If you plan to seek test-taking assistance from a private company, the answers to the following questions are important:

- What services do you offer students? Their parents?
- What do those services cost?
- What long-term value will there be for the student beyond higher test scores?
- What other benefits accrue to the students who use your services?
- What qualifications do your staff members have?
- Will you send out a brochure describing your services and fee structure?

Fill in the answers from each company you contact on the TEST PREPARATION SERVICES WORKSHEET on pages 82—83.

Testing Advice

The following advice will help you prepare to do well on these tests:

1. Do not overemphasize the importance of your scores to your future—especially if tests make you nervous. In other words, don't "psych yourself out" by thinking about them TOO much!

2. Learn relaxation techniques that you can use before and

during the test to stay calm and collected. Meditation, yoga, deep breathing or listening to a relaxing tape are all beneficial.

3. Understand the DIRECTIONS and FOLLOW THEM. For each test, find out if you will be penalized if you answer incorrectly.

4. Refer to a test preparation book (like those listed in our Resource List) to learn about the types of questions you will be asked. It's essential you understand what each category of question asks you to do. If you aren't sure what an "analogy" is, how can you draw one?

5. Prepare yourself physically. For several days before the test, get a normal amount of sleep and eat nourishing food. You can't spend the week before the tests cramming, drinking coffee, eating junk food and expect your body to repair the damage overnight. On the morning of the test, eat a good breakfast and exercise moderately.

6. Plan on working to the best of your ability, NOT BEYOND IT!

IMPORTANT NOTE: No matter how many books you read, tutors you hire or advice you listen to and follow, THERE IS NO GUARANTEE YOU WILL BE ABLE TO AFFECT YOUR TEST SCORES. But such preparation might well help you perform at least to the best of your ability.

What To Do When Your Scores Arrive

When you examine that first scoresheet, be sure you and your parents understand what it means. The testing service sends a written explanation with your results. If you and your parents read it thoroughly, but still feel like you're in the dark, contact either your guidance counselor, the testing service (see your Registration Bulletin) or a college admissions officer.

If Your Scores Are Disappointing

If you aren't happy with the results, don't despair. Remember: Test scores are only a *part* of the college admissions criteria. If you wish, you can arrange to re-take the test. You can also request a copy of your answer sheet from the testing service to check where you may have had difficulty. If you want further assistance before you try the test again, check the methods and resources suggested above. Identify subject areas where you may need help, and get it.

PARENTS

If you have followed your student's school testing history (which should be collected in the student's record file), you can make a realistic projection about possible college entrance testing results. Be reasonable with your expectations, and don't add to the student's stress level. If the student is disappointed with his or her scores, offer support and encouragement, NOT criticism!

PART TWO

The College Search

CHAPTER EIGHT

Shopping For Colleges

BOTH

The process of college selection is a complex one; there are many factors to be considered. As we've discussed in previous chapters, it is important to clarify the student's skill level; life style; personal, educational and career goals; and extracurricular interests. Other equally important selection factors—college location, size, housing, academic challenge and which majors and degrees are offered—need to be considered now. This chapter will guide you as you begin to shop for the colleges that meet your unique set of priorities.

In order for you to get the most out of this book and the planning process we have designed to help you, make sure you have completed all the exercises in Part 1; go back and do them now if you have not already done so. Like the grocery shopper, you need to have your academic and extracurricular shopping list in order *before* you start down the aisle. The shopper with a list is more likely to purchase what he or she needs and avoid impulse shopping or purchasing unnecessary items.

By the student's junior year of high school, it is time to consider what particular colleges have to offer and what your priorities are in selecting one. For most people, cost is a primary factor, though it shouldn't be the *main* determinant for selecting suitable colleges. Parents should have an accurate estimate of the yearly amount they can afford to contribute to the student's education. (See chapter 11—Planning Your Finances.)

STUDENT

Creating Your Shopping List

Use the books recommended in the College Shopping section of the Resource List at the back of this book to start collecting pre-campus visit information on colleges you are considering. Then use the College Shopping List on the next pages to determine which factors are important and list the essential information your research reveals. If you need more room, need to list more than six colleges or more factors that are important to you, simply recopy the List on separate sheets of paper, as many as you need.

Here's a sample of the entries for the mythical "State U," to show you how to get the most out of your Shopping List:

- **Location:** Medium (75,000)
- **Transportation:** 3 hrs. by bus; $32 round-trip fare
- **Campus Size/Description:** Large (18,000+); nice campus; can walk everywhere; bus service to downtown and other areas.
- **Academics:** Moderately challenging.
- **Required Test Scores:** SAT—500 (V)/600 (M); ACT—26; ATs—None required.
- **Expenses:** Tuition—$2,600; Room & Board—$2,900; Other Fees—Books, $300, Miscellaneous—$75.
- **Planned Majors Offered:** Biological Sciences; Pre-Med.

- **Housing and Other Facilities:** Male, female and co-ed dorms available; good library; new Bio-Med Building
- **How it meets student's learning style:** Atmosphere and size of classes perfect; matches well in all respects.

Before you start filling out your own List, you might find some explanation of the different types (classifications) of colleges helpful:

College is a generic term for a post-high school institution of advanced learning. Upon completion of your studies, you earn a bachelor 's degree in liberal arts, science, fine arts or engineering. These degrees usually can be completed with four years of study.

Community colleges (and ***junior colleges)*** offer two-year programs and usually serve a town or county. They generally cost less than four-year institutions. If you are considering completing two years at a community college and then transferring to a four-year school, be sure to check with the four-year school about their policies regarding transferring credits. Do this *before* you begin the two year program!

Private colleges obtain their primary funding from individuals (such as alumni—past graduates), businesses, foundations and grants. Some serve solely women or solely men; most are coeducational (serving both men and women). Some may focus on serving minorities; others may be sponsored by and stress the teachings of a particular religious sect or leader.

Public colleges receive their primary funding from the Federal and State governments. As a result, they generally cost less to attend, especially if the student is a resident of the state in which the college is located.

Liberal arts colleges generally offer four-year programs with a variety of courses and majors leaning toward a well-rounded, more "cultural" education. They grant Bachelor of Arts (A.B. or B.A.) and, sometimes, Bachelor of Science (B.S.) degrees.

COLLEGE SHOPPING LIST

	COLLEGE 1	COLLEGE 2	COLLEGE 3
Name			
Type of institution (2-year, 4-year, etc.)			
Location (Large City, medium city, small town, rural)			
Transportation (to and from)			
Campus Size (Large, medium, etc.)			
Academic Atmosphere (Challenging, Moderately challenging, relaxed)			

COLLEGE SHOPPING LIST (Continued)

	COLLEGE 1	COLLEGE 2	COLLEGE 3
Required Test Scores: SAT— ACT— AT—			
Expenses: Tuition Room & Board Other Fees			
Preferred Majors Offered			
Housing: Dorms/Residence Halls Off-campus Other Facilities			
How it meets my learning style			

COLLEGE SHOPPING LIST

	COLLEGE 4	COLLEGE 5	COLLEGE 6
Name			
Type of institution (2-year, 4-year, etc.)			
Location (Large City, medium city, small town, rural)			
Transportation (to and from)			
Campus Size (Large, medium, etc.)			
Academic Atmosphere (Challenging, Moderately challenging, relaxed)			

COLLEGE SHOPPING LIST (Continued)

	COLLEGE 4	COLLEGE 5	COLLEGE 6
Required Test Scores: SAT— ACT— AT—			
Expenses: Tuition Room & Board Other Fees			
Preferred Majors Offered			
Housing: Dorms/Residence Halls Off-campus Other Facilities			
How it meets my learning style			

Specialized institutions grant degrees in more specific programs of studies. An example would be an institute of mining and technology or a school of music.

Universities offer both undergraduate (Bachelor's degree) and graduate (Master's or Doctorate degrees) programs. A university often has more extensive research facilities, course offerings and professional schools (Law, Medicine, Journalism, etc.). Universities are often public institutions, but they can be private (as are all the Ivy League schools, for example).

Vocational-Technical schools/Technical colleges stress the employment of students upon graduation by providing the skills and technical base of knowledge that will help the student get a job.

After you have considered all the options listed above, try to pinpoint which types of colleges might interest you and begin filling in your college preferences on the Shopping List. (Hint: Try to include a local college that fits some or most of the factors detailed on your Shopping List. Research that college and schedule a visit to the campus (see chapter 10). Based on your first-hand experience, you'll be able to determine which book's ratings are most in "sync" with your own perceptions.

With the possible exception of your local college, complete the Shopping List prior to planning campus visits. Remember: Be a"choosy consumer"—if you don't know what you're shopping for, how will you ever find it?

PARENTS

You may choose to make up your own Shopping List to collect other information on each college that's important to *you*—a geographic profile of students on campus, the companies that interview and hire graduates from the college, the percentage of freshmen who actually graduate and the cost and tuition increases in recent years.

STUDENT

The Elimination Process

Start this process by researching six to ten colleges. This will help you get comfortable with the comparison process. Starting with fewer schools will narrow your target list too early; starting with more may overwhelm you. Next, look at the factors you wrote down on your Shopping List. Can you identify some obvious "likes" and "dislikes" about any of your six to ten schools? For example, one school may offer the major you want but be farther away than you'd like. Would you be comfortable visiting home only two or three times a year?

Continue both researching each school and weighing the information you obtain. Once you feel you've learned all you can about the colleges on your list from books and brochures, you must evaluate the schools. Are there enough significant "dislikes" to eliminate a college from your list before you visit? Then do so! By letting the "nays" take an early fall, you will continue to logically narrow your search to the top candidates.

PARENTS

Make sure you're aware of the factors that are important to the student. Participate in the process of identifying unacceptable characteristics and eliminating schools. Hint: A microcomputer is very useful for keeping track of your comparisons, since you will be making many revisions along the way. You may want to arrange your priorities on a spreadsheet so you can easily compare how each college stacks up.

STUDENT

Pre-Visit Preparation

You can improve your efficiency by writing down the precampus visit factors using a colored ink pen. Then, while you're on campus, use a regular pen to check off qualities on your List and to make brief notes to yourself. Review the priorities and needs you identified on your "Who Am I?" information sheet.

You'll continue to use your Shopping List as you visit your target schools. During your visit, take a few minutes to document your observations on how each college stacks up before you turn the key in the ignition to move out. Note the slightest thing that doesn't feel right and all the ones that *do* impress you about the school. It is amazing what you lose out of your memory bank by the time you get home. Keep as much data as possible written down on the Shopping List.

Remember: A campus visit and interview will be much more productive and rewarding if you and your parents do your homework *before* arriving on-campus.

Competitive Colleges

Competitive colleges are characterized by their difficult and lengthy admissions process and the high quality facilities and education they offer the exceptional students they accept. By definition, there are always far fewer places in the freshman class than students trying to get accepted at such schools. Competitive colleges may require better test scores on the SAT, ACT and Achievement Tests, higher grade point averages and class rank, more detailed application forms, and investigate you, your education and activities in greater detail than other schools.

Presuming you have the grades and other talents to be accepted, you may want to consider attending a competitive college if:

- You want to study with others who share your higher degree of intellectual curiosity and quest for knowledge.

- You wish to eventually gain admission to a competitive professional or graduate school.

- You are extremely bright and want the opportunity to pursue an undiluted course of programs and have more in-depth course offerings in your major.

• You want the opportunity to focus on subjects that will specifically prepare you for a high-powered career and/or very skilled or technical fields.

• You hope to leave college with the superior education and better career opportunities that a school with a top academic reputation may offer.

• You are capable of absorbing knowledge and have the motivation and self-discipline to maintain a high grade point average in a challenging environment.

• You seek the prestige inherent in such colleges.

• You seek the finest physical facilities—laboratories, libraries and studios—and access to high-caliber research centers.

Competitive colleges vary in the types of experiences and preparations they offer their students.

The high-end competitive liberal arts schools—such as Harvard, Princeton and Yale—generally offer challenging, quality courses in a broad variety of majors.

The high-end technological schools such as Massachusetts Institute of Technology (MIT), California Institute of Technology (Cal Tech) and Rochester Institute of Technology (RIT) offer many, if not all, of the same majors a liberal arts college would, but concentrate most of their resources on their scientific and engineering facilities and departments.

The same goes for competitive fine arts schools such as the Julliard School of Music, Pratt Institute, Bard College and the School of Visual Arts—they're poor choices for aspiring physicists, but the top of the heap for aspiring artists, actors, musicians, etc.

Some colleges or universities that would not necessarily be considered as competitive as a Princeton or MIT offer certain programs that are very prestigious and, hence, most competitive. For example, New York University (NYU) and the University of Southern California (USC) boast the two best-known programs for aspiring filmmakers. Northwestern University offers one of the most competitive communications programs in the United States. There are also smaller, regional liberal arts colleges—such as Amherst College in Massachusetts, Carleton College in Minnesota and Pomona College in California—that are highly competitive.

A final category of competitive schools is the United States military academies, such as the Air Force Academy, the U.S. Military Academy (West Point) and the U.S. Naval Academy (Annapolis). The U.S. government pays all educational expenses plus a salary to each cadet accepted, probably an important consideration for students unable to afford the superior education these schools provide.

There are some key differences between all other colleges and the military academies. First, though the latter measure potential students by all the usual admissions criteria, they place a much greater emphasis on the student's physical fitness (and require the student to undergo a complete physical. Otherwise qualified candidates *are* rejected if they fail that physical.) Second, the admissions process begins earlier—preliminary applications must be submitted in the student's junior year of high school. Third, the application process requires you to be nominated to the academy you wish to attend. Nominations may only be made by Congressmen, Senators, the Vice-President and President of the United States. Successful candidates are generally notified in the fall of their senior year.

If you have a clear-cut preference for a particular competitive college, inquire about ***early decision*** and ***early action*** possibilities. *Early decision* applications require you to apply earlier (usually in November) and, if you are accepted by the school, *to attend college there*. If *early action* is offered, you may apply by an even earlier deadline date. When you are informed of your acceptance, you are still allowed to apply to other colleges. But you must give the early action school your final decision in the spring, probably before the standard college response date.

Rolling admissions means that applications are processed as they come in. Generally, if a school offers rolling admissions, you will receive a response to your application much faster.

Be sure to apply to a ***safety school:*** one school to which you feel you will surely be accepted. To paraphrase: "An acceptance in hand is worth two in the bush."

Final comment: The more competitive the school, the more resourceful a student applicant has to be. If you are applying for a competitive school in a performing area like athletics or theater, provide a videotape or portfolio demonstrating your skills and talents. Mark on your calendar the dates when mid-senior-year grades must be mailed to these competitive schools. All the advice in Chapter 9—College Applications—applies doubly to you!

PARENTS

Admit and analyze your own emotional pulls toward a competitive or prestigious school and try to balance them with the student's needs. It is important to consider whether a school is a better buy academically and financially.

When (And If) To Hire A Private Consultant

While we feel that most families can plan together for an appropriate and high-quality college education, especially through the use of this book, a private college consultant may be helpful in some circumstances and for some families. If, for example, you've held all the family goal-setting and planning meetings and consulted with the high school guidance counselor, but the student is still very unclear about most of his or her educational priorities, you might consider contacting a consultant. Consultants can, for a fee, help focus on students' goals and suggest colleges suitable for them.

CONSULTANT SUMMARY WORKSHEET

	CONSULTANT 1	CONSULTANT 2	CONSULTANT 3
Name			
Address			
Telephone			
Contact			
Date Contacted			
Services:			

CONSULTANT SUMMARY WORKSHEET (Continued)

	CONSULTANT 1	CONSULTANT 2	CONSULTANT 3
Consultant's Qualifications			
Fees			
References			

Consultants can assist students with essay writing, resume preparation and interview techniques, as well as plan visits and schedule admissions interviews. The consultant can also help if a parent or student feels they need more information on application guidelines, admissions standards and the odds of "getting in" to a particular college. They can relieve families who are pressed for time by attending to the myriad details and follow-up inherent in the application process. Finally, if parents and student determine that specialized, impartial assistance is needed to pair the student who has unusual needs or preferences with an appropriate college or university, a consultant may be able to complete the search for you.

To locate a qualified consultant, ask your high school guidance counselor for a recommendation. And check your local telephone directory. But before you hire someone, ask the following questions. (Record answers on the Consultant Summary on pages 102 & 103):

1. What services will the consultant provide? Do those services match your student's needs? (If you have reviewed the process mapped out in this book, you should be able to determine at which points your student will need the consultant's help.)

2. What counseling background does the consultant and/or his or her staff have? What college admissions background?

3. What is the consultant's fee and for what services? (In our experience, consultants charge either by the hour—$50 and up—or on a flat fee basis—$1,000 to $2,500.)

4. What references can the consultant offer?

CHAPTER NINE

Applying To Colleges

STUDENT

Obtaining Catalogs And Application Materials

Once you've targeted the six to ten schools that interest you and seem to meet your priorities, check to see whether your high school guidance office has catalogs for those schools. Many public libraries also have collections of college catalogs. If a particular catalog is unavailable, write or call the college to request one. Addresses and telephone numbers for every college nationwide are in most of the college guidebooks listed on our Resource List. You can also find addresses and phone numbers in each city's telephone directory (many libraries have a collection of national directories) or in your high school guidance or career counseling office.

Just looking through a college's catalog may confirm your decision to keep the college on your target list or eliminate it from consideration. As you review each catalog, use your

Shopping List to determine how or whether each will meet your needs. What are the school's philosophy and goals in education? Does it offer the programs and activities you want? What does the campus look like in the pictures? (Keep in mind that colleges, not unexpectedly, put their best foot forward in the catalogs. But if you find the photos of the campus depressing—and that's the best they can show you!—you probably don't even want to visit.)

Many colleges now offer videotapes as well as printed catalogs, so request to see the video, too. Campus visits are costly and, in some cases, out of the question. Fully utilizing such preliminary information will help you stay selective.

If you telephone to ask for applications, record the school name, telephone number, the name of the person who spoke with you, his or her position and the date of the call on your Month-by-Month Planning Calendar (see chapter 12) and/or on your College Search Checklist printed on the inside back cover. Keeping this information is important. If you fail to receive promised materials, it will enable you to see how much time has passed since you made the request, quickly locate the college's phone number and contact the same person with questions. If you choose to write for applications, keep a copy of the letter in your record file, for the same reasons.

The application itself may also tell you something about this school and its standards. How much information are you asked to supply? Are there essay questions? How many? What kinds of questions are asked? A college application that asks for minimal information may indicate a more relaxed admissions procedure and lower admissions standards.

Filling Out Applications

Be sure to decide where you are going to apply early enough to allow several weeks to complete the applications. Better yet, try to leave a few months for the application process. Chances are you will have many other commitments during those weeks like school, jobs, activities and dates. APPLICATIONS ARE TIME CONSUMING. SAVE YOUR-

SELF GRIEF. START EARLY! *Colleges do not accept applications after their deadline. Period.*

Your resume, the "Who Am I?" worksheet (and possibly your parent's "Who Is Your Student?" worksheet) and the Priorities for College Selection list will make the application process much easier, so have them handy before you begin.

Read the directions and the application thoroughly before you begin to write. Duplicate the application at least once, so you can pencil in the information and think about all your answers before you type them onto the actual form. *The application is the first (and lasting) impression you'll be making on the admissions people who will decide your fate. Make the* right *impression—make sure your application is clearly and neatly presented.* Don't panic, you'll do fine. Just use a little extra care and thought.

Obtaining Letters Of Recommendation

Check instructions on each application form and note if you need letters of recommendation and from whom. Carefully choose who you ask to give you a recommendation—you want those teachers, employers, etc., of course, who will give you the most positive letters. And be considerate when you ask—teachers, counselors, neighbors and employers are busy; they may well be swamped with requests for recommendations from other students.

If more than one recommendation letter is required, select people who can comment on different aspects of you or your life—teachers of different subjects, an activity advisor or coach, etc. If possible, ask someone who's come to know you in a variety of settings—for example, your physics teacher, who is also your track coach.

Here are some suggestions to help you get the best possible letters of recommendation:

- Ask for the recommendation politely and let the people you ask know you appreciate the time and effort such letters take to properly prepare. ***Don't*** apologize for asking, but ***do*** be gracious and grateful.

• The earlier you ask for such letters, the better. But in no case allow less than two weeks for the writers to complete the recommendations. People become very upset when you force tight deadlines on them with little notice.

• Along with the recommendation form, make sure you give each invitee a correctly addressed and stamped envelope, so writers can simply mail the recommendation to the college when they have completed it. If you know to whom the letter should be addressed, make sure your writers know—it's better than addressing the letter to "Dear Sir/Madam."

• Provide the writers with a copy of your resume to prompt their own memories of your time together and give them a fuller picture of you and your accomplishments. Some people also appreciate a brief note (even if you see them in person) outlining what *you* think should be included in the letter.

• If you haven't seen the person in a long time (your tenth grade teacher in whose class you were really excited and did your best work), refresh his or her memory with samples of your work from the class or a description of your work.

An Easy Way To Write Essays

Many colleges require you to complete one or more essay questions as part of the application process. If any of your selections do, you need to carefully plan your answers, since they are often given great weight by admissions offices. Allow several weeks to accumulate ideas, outline and write your first draft, revise and refine it, and review it with family members and others.

Check each application you need to complete. Do several ask many of the same or similar questions? (More than 100 colleges use a common application form for admissions.) If so, you might decide to write on the same topic for more than one school, saving you time and energy.

Search for an essay question that will allow you to write about yourself and the unique properties, talents and abilities you can offer that school. Review your "Who Am I?" worksheet and take the opportunity to revise or add to the essay based on that review. Ask your parents, friends and/or teachers for their input—not only about what they feel you've accomplished (by now you should know that), but also about how they see you as a person.

Once you've completed this preparation, you're ready to put your thoughts on paper. Here's a method—a proven success—that will make your job much easier:

Step One

Read the essay question. List any and all ideas that come to mind, then put the question and your notes away for the day.

Step Two

When you return to your task, look at what you listed and extract the best ideas, then list as many details about those ideas as you can. Then, again, put the essay away for the day. (You should only have spent an hour or so on both steps so far, so don't think something is wrong because you've completed them so quickly!)

Step Three

(You can put your ideas in logical order now—creating an outline for your essay—or simply move on to the next step and worry about organizing your essay later.) Write out, as quickly as you can, all the ideas you wish to express. If new ideas come as you write, be sure to include them on paper. This is a first draft—the language is *supposed* to be "rough." So *don't* worry now about complete sentences, order, grammar or punctuation. (You can think about them later. Honest!) Just get your thoughts on paper. If you get stuck at any point, just keep writing your last thought over and over until a new one comes. Write for at least 15 minutes.

Step Four

At this point you can "cut and paste" (literally cutting the paper apart and taping the thoughts or paragraphs back together in the order you want them) or move the ideas around on the page into any order that seems to work. You can also begin to work at cleaning up sentence structure, grammar, punctuation, etc.. If you are one of those people who keeps working on essays forever (or procrastinates forever), SET A DEADLINE NOW FOR COMPLETING THE ESSAY AND THE APPLICATION, AND STICK TO IT. If you think it will help, ask a parent or friend to remind you about your deadlines...frequently.

Step Five

Instead of the blank page you started with, you now have an abundance of essay material ready to shape into final form. At this point, spend more time honing the first and last paragraphs and finalize sentence structure, grammar, punctuation and style throughout. Continue to concentrate on expressing the "real you" in the essay. Ask your parents, teachers or counselor (or anyone you trust) to read the entire essay and give you their criticisms. Proofread the final draft one last time, then type or write it on the application form.

Don't stop now. *Be sure to proofread* *again* *for errors (spelling, typos, grammar) on the application form and essay before you mail them.*

Did you sign the application form? Have you enclosed a check for the required fees? A self-addressed, stamped post-card? Did you make a copy of the application and the check to save in your record file in case someone loses one or both? If you can answer "yes" to all of the above for every application you've completed, your job is done.

PARENTS

Writing applications often requires old-fashioned parental guidance, particularly to help students plan the several hours of work most require and meet the stringent deadlines. We suggest that students allow several weeks, if not a few months, to complete applications. They should also allow two more weeks for people to write their recommendations, and another two weeks for the school to process completed applications. The student may need your help in marking deadlines on the calendar, planning several short application-writing times (on the calendar!) and sticking to the deadlines.

You can also support the student by writing a list of his or her personality traits, personal strengths and attributes. If possible, each parent (and other concerned planners) should compile a separate list. (Is it worth your time? We all love to hear what people appreciate about us, especially when it's on paper and we can see it again and again. We know kids who have pinned their parents' lists to their bulletin boards.)

Another supportive activity is to encourage your student to compile that resume. It will save time in the application process and start him or her on the right track towards a successful education and career. If your student has already compiled a resume, read it to be sure it is complete.

If you feel it is appropriate and you are willing, offer some behind-the-scenes assistance. Getting telephone numbers and addresses of colleges, typing letters, resumes or completed applications, and proofreading any of the above are a big help to a student, especially one who's feeling a little overwhelmed by the task at hand. It is important to have students request catalogs and applications themselves and prepare their own applications, but clerical assistance and feedback is a welcome relief.

If you are not yet committed to helping your student complete his or her college applications, remember: Your positive support and input are really needed now. Your student may not express it, but he or she will appreciate it!

CHAPTER TEN

Visiting Campuses

BOTH

When To Plan The Visit

The first question students usually ask is, "Do I really have to go?" Followed almost immediately by "Do I have to bring my parents?" Pardon the pun, but,"the eyes have it." Our advice is "yes" in both cases, particularly if it is a school with which everyone is unfamiliar, one that is quite a distance from home, or one that has already shown some interest in recruiting the student.

Casual campus visits can begin as early as ninth or tenth grade. Pick a college close to home where the student can attend a concert or homecoming event. Appointments with admissions offices are not necessary during these early visits.

In the eleventh and twelfth grades, campus visits should be carefully planned well in advance—it's time to get serious. To save on expenses, try coordinating campus visits with your regular vacation(s). To save time and allow the greatest family participation, use weekends and school breaks.

For each planned visit, start by deciding who will go. Next, set firm dates for the trip and make appointments with the college admissions office for an interview with a counselor. Most counselors' calendars are quickly filled up as application deadlines near, so telephone early for an appointment. Reservations to stay overnight in a campus residence hall should also be made in advance.

STUDENT

Don't bring any friends along—they may influence your opinions and your ability to look at the school objectively.

And be patient with your parents. They may not know the latest language or the trendiest way to do some things, but they are doing what they hope is the best thing for you. You may share some special moments and create some memories for the future.

PARENTS

Be braced for the fact that your student may feel that visiting college campuses is a waste of time. One student hoping to attend a competitive school told us he was so into the "present" that campus visits meant he would miss parties, sports events, etc. He was miserable on the first trip he and his family took, but his parents persevered anyway, and he was eventually grateful that they did. As he started winnowing down his target list, he was able to compare schools based on his own observations. He felt more confident that he had made a sound, informed decision.

(Incidentally, the school that he had originally placed at the top of his list was a disappointment in person, nothing like the place his reading had led him to envision. Once he visited the campus, he decided not to apply there.)

A small parental reward for getting your student to visit *several* campuses—later in life, there will be less chance of him or her lamenting, "Gee, I wish I had gone to Mega U."

What To Do During Your Visit

STUDENT

If you have time before your interview, take a walk around the campus when you first arrive. Look around. Listen. What do the buildings and grounds look like? Observe the students. Read a couple of issues of the student newspaper. If you can find one, browse through a faculty publication.

If you'd like to talk to some of the students but feel hesitant, just ask one for directions. That's a great way to start a casual informational conversation. As you look around and talk to students, ask yourself: "Can I imagine myself living here for eight months? For four years?" Take your "Who Am I?" information with you, and keep in mind how you learn best. Do you need quiet or music when you study? Do you study in the morning or night? Do you learn well in large lectures or smaller groups? Rate the facilities according to *your* needs and by *your* standards.

PARENTS

You should do many of the same things as your student. Observe the buildings, grounds and facilities to see how well they are maintained. This could be an indication of the financial health of the school and the image it projects. Pick up a college newspaper or a faculty newspaper. What do they tell you about this school? At the admissions office, inquire about faculty education and teaching experience, percentage of full-time staff and the qualifications of those teaching freshman classes. Then ask yourselves: "Can I imagine my child living here for eight months of the year? For four years?"

BOTH

Before the interview, take a campus tour, which can usually be arranged through the admissions office. Often these tours are conducted by students, which gives you a chance to really learn about the place. The students are very proud of their school and knowledgeable not only about the campus and town, but also about what the school, its classes and social life are *really* like.

STUDENT

Check out the following facilities while you are on tour. Don't forget to keep your learning needs and style uppermost in your mind. Select colleges with facilities that seem appropriate to you and your needs.

Classroom buildings

Classroom buildings generally are assigned by department (for example, Biological Sciences Building or Fine Arts Building). If possible, arrange (through the admissions office) to observe a class and meet a professor. If a laboratory is important in your studies, go see one. Look at the equipment. Is it up-to-date and sophisticated? Or old and elementary?

Housing

Dormitories and residence halls may be all-male, all-female or coed (both). Are the dorm facilities all owned by the college or privately owned and operated? Ask about the availability and quality of dormitory space for incoming freshmen. If housing is "tight," find out if there is a housing application deadline and don't miss it! Find out how roommates are assigned and whether you can indicate preferences for people with similar study and life habits. (If you like to study all night, imagine how difficult it would be to share a room with someone who rises with the sun.)

Library

Where is the library? Is it is well-lit, warm and conducive to the way you like to study? Does the library staff appear knowledgeable and willing to help?

Bookstores

This one is fun! Really shop the bookstores. Observe how they stock the shelves by academic department. Look through a few texts and check the prices. You'll probably see some school-spirit items. If it's in your budget and you really like the campus, treat yourself to a momento—a notebook, pennant, sweatshirt or a present for a brother or sister.

Performing arts center

Is there one? Are there cultural series, performances and films offered with reduced admission costs or with costs included in your tuition? Are there performing opportunities for the student interested in music or theater?

Athletic facilities

Make sure you tour the gym(s) and athletic fields. For students with athletic ambitions, there are strict NCAA guidelines if you are being recruited or are an athletic scholarship candidate. The athletic department should inform you of your rights in advance of your visit. If they don't, some of the books found under "Athlete's Information" in the Resource List explain NCAA rules.

Student Center

Spend some time at the student center (student union). What's it used for? Are there many people there? What are they doing? Do they look happy, contented, frazzled, glum? The best people-watching is generally at the student center. Sit up and take notice!

Dining halls

Where are they? How far from the freshmen dorms? Sample a meal. Would you enjoy eating there daily? Are there meal servers? Are they pleasant?

Restaurants

Are there nearby restaurants for after-hours survival food like burgers and pizza?

Museums and galleries

Are there any on campus or within walking distance? Do they appear welcoming and appealing to students?

Student Health Center

It's a rare student who stays completely healthy during four years of college. Make sure the college has the professionals and facilities to help when you do become ill.

Financial aid

Go to the financial aid office and pick up any necessary materials that you were unable to get at the admissions office. If materials you need are not yet available, ask that your name and address be placed on their mailing list.

Shopping

Are there stores where basic essentials may be purchased? It shouldn't be necessary to bring a year's supply of toothpaste or laundry detergent from home.

Recreational activities

If social life is important to you, make sure there are movie theaters, recreational facilities, and nightlife nearby. Are there buses or other means of transportation to different parts of town or to nearby towns?

If you follow the same basic routine from campus to campus, you'll get a fairer and more accurate comparison of schools. This will eliminate the guesswork. When you do make that final decision, trust your instincts.

The Admissions Interview

To prepare for your admissions interview, read the college's publications thoroughly. Make a list of questions about the school itself and the admissions process based on information that is NOT provided in the catalog. Make good use of the interviewer's time. If you have not yet sent your high school records to the college, bring a copy of your resume and high school transcript to the interview. Dress neatly and respectfully.

The interview is generally held without the parents present. Usually, parents introduce themselves, exchange pleasantries and then excuse themselves to explore the campus on their own. They may ask questions after the interview. If, however, it appears to be an informal interview and parents *are* invited to sit in, make sure you all have agreed to this plan in advance of the visit.

During the interview, stay as relaxed as possible. Eye contact and a positive facial expression can make you and the admissions officer more comfortable (but don't be plastic). *Remember: You are interviewing the school as well as being interviewed. Get the information you need.*

One last point: Please be sure to thank interviewers for their time. If they thank you for your time, it is an indication of concern and respect for their students.

Orientation Sessions

Once you have made your big decision and have been accepted by a college, plan to attend an orientation session. During the orientation you may do some pre-testing to determine which classes you should take and at which level. You may register for those classes. In addition, there are opportunities to meet other incoming freshmen and begin new friendships during planned activities. Do this even if you made a campus visit earlier. Different colleges have different orientation programs, all providing a good opportunity to take the initial steps into the college environment in which you'll be spending the next four years.

PARENTS

Sometimes parents are invited to this orientation. These sessions are wonderfully informative about student life and offer a perfect time to assess the student's room-furnishing needs and what can be supplied from home. Be sure to pick up and use a parent's handbook if one is available.

CHAPTER ELEVEN

Planning Your Finances

BOTH

At the beginning of this book, we suggested that each planner review the student's educational assets and liabilities. Likewise, the first step in planning how to *pay* for the college you select is a review of the family's financial assets and liabilities.

What are parents willing and able to contribute to the student's college expenses—particularly in the first year? What can the student afford to contribute? Students need to know now what financial responsibility they will bear for their education. The object of this important analysis is to determine the cold, hard, dollar-and-cents reality the family must be prepared to face. The statement, "We'll help you as much as we can," indicates support and parental sacrifice, but doesn't tell the student enough. Will the parents provide $1,000 or $10,000 per year?

PARENTS

Assessing your finances is a difficult and somewhat frightening process, because in addition to discovering what you *do have* financially, you may discover what you *do not have*. The best advice we can offer is simply to begin your financial planning as early as possible.

Keep in mind that this may be the first time your student has been included in a major family financial matter. Students often feel guilty about placing an additional financial burden on their parents—they need honest feedback, so they can make choices that are realistic for themselves. Please be sensitive to them. If you are not honest with your student, you'll just add to his or her confusion and guilt. As difficult as this discussion may be, it *is* an important factor in the student's continued growth and emerging independence.

STUDENT

Discussing finances may be the most emotional conversation you engage in during the college planning process. Your parents may come to a painful realization—even though they want the very best for you, they may not be able to afford it. And may even feel guilty about not being able to offer you more financial support.

If you're financing your education on your own, don't despair! There are plenty of options for getting the help you need.

BOTH

No matter what your financial status, do not make *any* determinations of what you can or cannot afford until you have reviewed your finances, applied for whatever aid you can and received the final results!

PARENTS

Review what property you own, available equity in your home, investments, stocks, bonds, insurance policies, bank accounts, retirement accounts, your monthly budget and known future financial obligations. When you have this information in order and on paper, see how much money can be contributed to your student's education from your personal resources. But don't sell or re-finance anything yet! It is advisable not to implement any major changes in your financial holdings until you have checked out all the implications of anticipated changes with your accountant (and made sure you really do have to contribute that much yourself).

Do You Need A Financial Planner?

If you feel you need help with this analysis, locate a reputable accountant or financial planner by looking in your local Yellow Pages or talking with friends or colleagues. Professionals can assist you in many ways and really make the task easier. We have developed a list of questions that you can ask any financial planning firm to ensure you are receiving the best possible advice (and a worksheet on which to summarize their answers):

1. Do they offer a free initial inquiry meeting? (Such a meeting is the best way to "check out" any consultant.)

2. How long has the firm been in business? (Five to 15 years indicates an established track record.) Contact your local Better Business Bureau to confirm this information and further investigate a potential planner.

3. Exactly what services does the firm offer? What programs or plans do they sell? Who is the firm's broker/dealer? (Information on broker/dealers can be obtained by reading *Forbes* and the *Wall Street Journal.*)

FINANCIAL PLANNER WORKSHEET

	PLANNER 1	PLANNER 2	PLANNER 3
Name			
Address			
Telephone			
Contact			
Date Contacted			
Services:			

FINANCIAL PLANNER WORKSHEET (Continued)

	PLANNER 1	PLANNER 2	PLANNER 3
Years in business Credentials Plans they sell			
Broker/Dealer Years experience Credentials			
Fee Structure Total approx. cost			
Inital mtg. free?			
College planning experience?			

4. What is the planner's background and credentials? How long has he or she been in the business? Does he or she have a license to sell insurance? A Series 7 credential to sell stocks, bonds, limited partnerships and annuities? Is he or she a Certified Financial Planner?

5. What is the fee structure for services? Financial planning can be based on three different types of fee structure:

a. A ***straight fee*** for a full financial assessment or to help solve specific problems (like financing your student's education);

b. A ***straight commission*** arrangement, applicable if you purchase products from the firm (such as insurance or stocks);

c. ***Fee plus commission***—you pay a fee for the plan and commissions on what you purchase.

A word of advice: Be sure the consultant is experienced in college financial planning, and ask in advance what you will be charged for all services you plan to utilize. If you are considering hiring such a financial planner, use the worksheet on pages 124 & 125 to summarize your research on those you contact.

STUDENT

You should research the costs of the colleges to which you wish to apply. List budget items for each college in the chart on the next page. [Before you calculate the costs of tuition, find out if the college (if it is out of state) offers a reciprocity agreement, allowing you to pay tuition similar to what you'd pay at a college in your home state.]:

	LOW COST	HIGH COST
TUITION	______	______
ROOM & BOARD	______	______
BOOKS AND SUPPLIES	______	______
TRANSPORTATION (HOME TO SCHOOL)	______	______
MEDICAL & HEALTH INSURANCE	______	______
PERSONAL EXPENSES		
Clothing	______	______
Room Furnishings	______	______
Social/Recreational	______	______
Personal Care (hair, toothpaste)	______	______
Laundry	______	______
Telephone (include long distance)	______	______
Snacks	______	______
Transportation around Campus	______	______
Sports or Lab Fees	______	______

In order to get a better feel for your normal monthly expenses, record all of them (whether paid by your parents or you) for a period of one month. Include every penny—from sodas to greeting cards. If you have not done this before, we guarantee some surprises about "where the money goes!" If you don't think this is important now, just wait until you have spent the entire personal allowance for your freshman year in the first three months!

PARENTS

Record and examine your family's expenditures to determine where some unforeseen dollars may be "found." This is also an excellent opportunity to "role model" some valuable money management techniques that we suggested to your student in the above section.

Try to creatively help your student learn how to budget and spend money wisely. Teach him or her to take pride in identifying products of good value, purchasing bargains and comparison shopping.

An especially helpful technique, we have found, is to start the student on a cash budget—place the actual dollars in envelopes marked with each expense and the amount budgeted per week or month. During high school, students can learn to budget money for clothing, entertainment, automobile expenses (like gasoline), personal grooming and "extras." Nothing teaches a teenager the value of careful budgeting better than an empty gasoline tank, an empty auto budget envelope and a week left before "pay day."

After your student has successfully learned to manage real dollars, start a checking account in the student's name or encourage him or her to start his or her own during high school.

There are two additional suggestions we think will help the student become more responsible with his or her spending money. The first is for parents to set the basic purchase price for an item. If the student wants to pay more for that item, the difference comes out of his or her pocket. For example, you may offer to pay $20 for a "basic" pair of jeans. If the student wants to spend $40 for a pair of "designer" jeans, he or she will have to budget his or her own money to pay the difference. Before you establish such "norms," however, be sure you realistically assess the lifestyle to which your student has already become accustomed. If designer clothes are already the norm, you've already established a high spending pattern and shouldn't "downgrade" the budget now.

Second, students also need to develop good savings habits. Let them begin to save for their own education. Parents can then offer an incentive plan for saving for college. For example, you may offer to match—dollar-for-dollar—every dollar your student saves. (You can lower or raise this matching ratio according to your own means.) This may also serve as an enforced savings plan for you.

BOTH

The paperwork for financial aid, including the family income tax, financial aid forms and bank loan applications, takes a lot of time to complete. Use the "What's The Plan?" sheets in Chapter 13 to establish a shared responsibility for gathering the necessary financial aid information. Fill in deadline dates on the College Search Information Checklist on the inside back cover of this book.

Finding The Aid You Need

By now, your research and analysis should have given you a good idea about college costs and the ability of your family's resources to meet them. If you're still wondering where the "shortfall" can be made up, it's time to look for additional sources of funding. The first thing you should check is whether you qualify for financial aid.

Obtaining financial aid is not a mystical process, but it is definitely a confusing one. Complicated by the myriad of agencies and forms involved, applying for financial aid can be a mind-boggling project; and there is no *one* place to go to get all the answers. In addition, it is a constantly changing process, due to congressional and legislative action and changes in government policy. You should refer to Chapter 13 to begin deciding which family member will complete each financial planning task.

The best place to start learning about financial aid is from your high school counselor. It is also definitely worth your time to study at least one book from the Resource List early in your planning process, particularly if you are unfamiliar with the sources for financial aid and the terms and criteria involved. If the student is a woman or minority, there are directories available that list financial aid sources for these special groups (see the Resource List).

Ask your high school's guidance counselor for suggestions on scholarship opportunities. Numerous organizations and businesses offer scholarships for a variety of purposes and reasons. Find out about local scholarship dollars for which you may qualify.

Completing Your Family Financial Statement

Searching for financial aid will require you to complete a family financial statement. You can obtain the necessary packet from your high school guidance office or by writing American College Testing for a Family Financial Statement (FFS)—ACT Student Need Analysis Services, PO Box 4006, Iowa City, IA 52243, or The College Board for a Financial Aid Form (FAF)—College Scholarship Service, CN 6300, Princeton, NJ 08541.

Though many colleges will accept either of these two forms, check with the individual schools to which you are applying to make sure you're supplying the form they prefer.

There are also state-sponsored financial aid programs. You can apply for this additional aid by checking the appropriate box on your FFS or FAF form or obtain state forms from your high school guidance office. The U.S. Department of Education divides their financial assistance offices by region. You can find out the region in which you live and the regional office address and telephone number through the guidance office, too.

If you need assistance in filling out the financial aid forms, ask your high school guidance counselor. A videotape may be available at the school, or a local cable TV station may provide some programming on the subject.

Financial Aid From The College

Based on your family's income, assets and other factors, each college will calculate the amount you are expected to pay. If your expected family contribution is less than the total cost of attending that college, the financial aid office will consider you for some form of financial aid package, which may consist of any or all of three components:

- **Scholarships and grants:** The most desirable, because the money will not have to be repaid.

- **Work-study:** Jobs are provided for the student to work 4-20 hours per week.

- **Loans:** These must be repaid along with accrued interest. Generally parents are asked to co-sign on the loans or take them out in their names for the student.

Each college determines how much it will make available to each applicant and the particular mix of above components, based on their available assets and the requests for aid by all students. Seemingly similar colleges may provide you with very different aid packages, so it is advantageous to apply for aid at every college you are considering. You should also be aware that you must generally re-apply for aid each year. For best results, apply as soon as possible after January 1.

Remember: The student can assist in paying some college tuition and expenses by getting a part-time job while in high school and starting to save for college.

Incurring loans to finance a college education may be the only way to make ends meet, but this step should not be taken lightly or without fully understanding the future cost of repayment. For example, a student who borrows $3,000 per year for four years accumulates a debt of $12,000...plus interest. That's comparable to buying another car or the down payment on another house! You must consider what the family or the student can afford to pay back when the loan comes due.

(If the interest rate is 8%, and the debt is paid off over 10 years in 120 equal payments, each monthly payment is $145.60, not an insignificant amount! Over the repayment period the total amount paid will be $17,472, including interest expense of $5,472. The tax consequences of this interest should be researched with your accountant. Think now about how this monthly payment will affect the student's life as a newly graduated employee or the parents' life if they take out the loan.)

If you are fortunate enough to have extra years to plan ahead for financing an education, *don't stop here!* Examine the two hypothetical savings tables (on the following pages) that illustrate the benefits of saving earlier in the student's life (prepared for us by financial planner Mary Kusske at Judith Brown & Associates in Edina, Minnesota). Both illustrations assume:

1. Each family currently has $5,000 set aside in a college fund;
2. The parents will provide 100% of the cost of college;
3. An estimated annual college cost of $7,000;
4. An annual inflation rate of 5%.

The first analysis is for a family with two children—one graduating this year (a 12th grader), the second in two years (a 10th grader).

The second analysis, again for two children, presumes the first is currently in 7th grade, the second in 1st grade.

EDUCATION FUNDING ANALYSIS I

Year	Number of Children in School	Cost in Today's Dollars	Total Inflated Need	Capital Need @ 10.00%
1987	0	0	0	$47,702
1988	1	$7,000	$7,350	52,472
1989	1	7,000	7,718	49,634
1990	2	14,000	16,207	46,108
1991	2	14,000	17,017	32,891
1992	1	7,000	8,934	17,462
1993	1	7,000	9,381	9,381
1994	0	0	0	0
1995	0	0	0	0
1996	0	0	0	0
1997	0	0	0	0
Totals	8	$56,000	$66,606	--------

Future education costs may be met by:

1. Investing a lump sum of capital.
   Initial capital required: $47,702

2. Depositing to a savings or investment fund monthly.
   Monthly deposit required: $663

3. Combining present fund with monthly deposits
   Initial college fund balance: $5,000
   Monthly additions needed: $594

4. Paying educational expenses with taxable, out-of-pocket income.
   Total of payments: $66,606

EDUCATION FUNDING ANALYSIS II

Year	Number of Children in School	Cost in Today's Dollars	Total Inflated Need	Capital Need @ 10.00%
1987	0	0	0	$35,455
1988	0	0	0	39,000
1989	0	0	0	42,900
1990	0	0	0	47,190
1991	0	0	0	51,909
1992	0	0	0	57,100
1993	1	7,000	9,381	62,810
1994	1	7,000	9,850	58,772
1995	1	7,000	10,342	53,815
1996	1	7,000	10,859	47,820
1997	0	0	0	40,656
1998	1	7,000	11,972	44,722
1999	1	7,000	12,571	36,025
2000	1	7,000	13,200	25,799
2001	1	7,000	13,860	13,860
2002	0	0	0	0
Totals	8	$56,000	$92,034	--------

Future education costs may be met by:

1. Investing a lump sum of capital.
   Initial capital required: $35,455

2. Depositing to a savings or investment fund monthly.
   Monthly deposit required: $296

3. Combining present fund with monthly deposits
   Initial college fund balance: $5,000
   Monthly additions needed: $254

4. Paying educational expenses with taxable, out-of-pocket income.
   Total of payments: $92,034

PART THREE

Charting Your Progress

CHAPTER TWELVE

Student Planning Calendar

This is a summary of the many tasks we've discussed throughout the book. Most of the information should be entered on your College Search Checklist, the family calendar or in the appropriate section of the next chapter ("What's the Plan?"), which summarizes your family's assignment of responsibility for each of these tasks. In a few cases, space for entering information right on this calendar has been provided. Whatever form or format your family chooses to use, make sure all appropriate information on the search process and the colleges to which the student is applying is organized, kept up-to-date and frequently reviewed.

You may wish to "check off" each item on this Calendar as it's accomplished and/or note the completion date beside each. This will help you keep track of everything you need to do and make sure you don't skip any steps along the way.

9TH GRADE

August—September

• Establish a permanent school record file at home. Review and understand report cards and standardized test scores. Also include any awards, honors or records of other accomplishments. (Chapter 6).

September—October

• Discuss educational goals, academic strengths and weaknesses. (Chapters 2-4).

• Determine where to get academic assistance, if needed. (Chapter 7)

• Explore and begin to plan high school courses now. This will help you avoid playing catch up later. Changes can always be made in the future.

• Note high school registration dates in your school calendar.

• Mark school conference dates on the family calendar:

Guidance counselor appt. : Date:________ Time:________

Fall teachers' conference : Date:________ Time:________

Spring teachers' conference : Date:________ Time:________

• Share goals and academic plans with key teachers and the guidance counselor at conference time. Doing this makes for a more informative conference.

Academic goals shared Date:________________________________

With whom?____

Results or comments from teachers or counselor :

Thoughts of my own :

My parents comments or ideas :

• Discuss current extracurricular activities. Plan which you want to continue and which new ones you might want to explore.

January-May

• Start (probably in concert with your parents) a college financial plan. (Chapter 11)

• Experiment with and explore learning and activities outside of the classroom. Use this time as an opportunity to try new things, such as a summer computer camp or a program at a local museum. (Chapter 5)

June

• Save samples of the year's school work—writing assignments, math tests, art projects, sports videos, clippings, etc.—which may later prove invaluable. Use your file or keep a large folder labelled by grade. (Chapter 6)

10TH GRADE

September—June

• Using your high school registration guide, look for challenging options such as honors programs, gifted programs, and possibilities like creative writers' workshops that may be offered in your local community.

• Keep your record file up to date—enter all report cards, test scores, awards, honors and records of other accomplishments. (Chapters 4 and 13) Make sure your family assigns responsibility for this important project.

• *Be sure there are dates on all materials placed in your file. Always use your complete legal name, not your nickname, when preparing records. These are two very simple but extremely valuable reminders.*

Spring (March—June)

• Meet with your school guidance counselor, if you are considering applying to competitive colleges. It's important that you register for the correct classes, know which pre-college tests must be taken and when. (Chapters 7 and 8)

• Review the family financial plan. (Chapter 11)

June

• One half of the student's academic high school career has been completed.

11TH GRADE

This is the most important year for college planning by a high school student. Be sure you have read Part One of this book before you continue with the following activities in Part Two and Three.

June—August

• Review your academic and activity plans for the coming year.

September

• Attend a college fair one evening (parents and student). In addition to individual college representatives answering questions and handing out materials, look for sessions on financial aid and college admissions procedures. Read Chapter 6 before you go to any fair and before you meet with any admissions people visiting your high school. (Chapter 11)

• Put college entrance test dates on the family calendar and register on time for these exams in the high school guidance office or through the appropriate testing service. (Chapters 7 and 9)

October

• Finalize your financial plan. This could be the most difficult and lengthy step in the college planning process. (Chapters 11 and 13)

• Seriously research all scholarship resources. This process, performed systematically, could provide money for your education. Start by asking your high school guidance office for scholarship materials. Scholarships are offered by colleges, businesses, service organizations, local clubs and the military. (Chapters 11 and 13)

Scholarships to work on:

Name and address: ______________________________

______________________ Date inquiry made: __________

Name and address: ______________________________

______________________ Date inquiry made: __________

Name and address: ______________________________

______________________ Date inquiry made: __________

Name and address: ______________________________

______________________ Date inquiry made: __________

• Borrow or purchase a book on college majors. (Chapter 14)

November

• Prepare a personal resume now. (Chapters 6 and 13)

• Research career interests. (Chapters 5 and 14)

• Determine if a competitive college is a primary goal. (Chapters 6 and 14)

• Decide if it's necessary to broaden and strengthen certain aspects of your life to assist in the personal development necessary for a competitive school environment. In certain parts of the country, this could involve a move to a preparatory school, European travel and/or other civic and cultural enrichment. (Chapters 2-5 and 14) It is important to know who the competition is and how to best represent yourself in the admissions process. Do not be naive.

November—August

• Formally and informally visit the colleges on your Shopping List. Fill in the list before you visit. When the visit is over, record your observations in a different color ink. Plan to use short breaks from school or family vacations. (Chapters 8 and 10)

Note: Do not disregard the importance of saving names and addresses of the people you met. They can really help later when you apply to (and hopefully end up attending) that school.

April—May

• Send for information from colleges of definite interest to you. (Chapters 9 and 13 and the College Search Information Checklist on the inside back cover of this book)

• If you score well on your college entrance exams, prepare to receive an onslaught of college mailings. This is *their* attempt to recruit *you!* Each one wants to get your attention early. Set guidelines for sorting out this material;

determine which information to save and which to pitch. (Chapters 1-8)

May—June

• Update your records. (Chapter 6)

• Update your resume. (Chapter 6)

August

• Assign the remaining "What's The Plan?" tasks. (Chapter 13)

12TH GRADE

By this time, you should have read this entire book... perhaps more than once! Students and parents who have completed Planning Calendars for grades 9-11 should have already completed many of the following steps.

August—September

• Determine which books you need. (Chapter 14) Borrow them from the library or purchase them at your local bookstore.

• If you have not already done so, assign all remaining "What's the Plan?" tasks. (Chapter 13) Please allocate enough family communication time to research the dates by which these tasks should be completed and to assign these fairly.

• Select five to ten colleges that appeal to you and appear to meet your needs. Mark them on your College Shopping List . (Chapter 8)

• Send for information and applications. (Chapter 9) Use the inside back cover of this book to record where you have inquired and on what date.

• Plan campus visits. (Chapter 10)

• Check with your high school guidance office for information on tuition reciprocity available with other states. (Usually available in those adjoining your state's borders.)

• Determine which tests are required by the colleges on your Shopping List and when each college must receive the test results. Plan your testing schedule. Enter appropriate dates on the College Search Checklist and the family calendar. (Chapter 7)

• Check on test dates and locations in the guidance office. Put the test registration dates along with the actual test dates on the family calendar (and/or in the spaces below):

Test:____________________ Date(s):____________________

Location:____

Test:____________________ Date(s):____________________

Location:____

Test:____________________ Date(s):____________________

Location:____

Test:____________________ Date(s):____________________

Location:____

• Many colleges will be sending representatives to your school to meet with interested and prospective students. These visits are publicized through the guidance office. Take advantage of these opportunities to meet with knowledgeable admissions people, especially if they represent a school you are interested in attending.

October

• If you are applying to competitive schools, notify your guidance counselor. This kind of application will require more time to process. Ask how much time the counselor will need to process your completed application so that it will arrive at the college before the deadline date. (Chapters 8 and 9):

Bring applications to my counselor _____ weeks in advance of deadline date.

• Register for test-taking sessions in the guidance office. (Chapter 7)

• Determine where you want test scores to be sent. Indicate those schools on the form available at registration. (Many schools prefer that the test scores be sent directly from the testing center.) Keep copies of your test scores in your record file. (Chapters 6 and 7)

• Inquire whether your high school offers extra classes in test preparation and/or essay writing. Sign up for them if you feel you need the help. (Chapter 7)

• Put college application deadline dates on your family calendar or the College Search Checklist you've made up for each college in which you're interested. (Chapter 9)

• Plan any remaining campus visit dates. (Chapter 10)

• Check the housing availability for freshman at the colleges where you are applying. Occasionally, residence hall space is at a premium and may be "first come, first served." Fill in pertinent information on the next page.

College name: ______________________________

Date application sent: ______________________________

College name: ______________________________

Date application sent: ______________________________

College name: ______________________________

Date application sent: ______________________________

• If you need letters of recommendation, complete your resume, then ask those persons from whom you'd like letters to write them. Give your letter writers at least two weeks. (Chapters 6 and 9)

• If you are applying for early decision at a college, the application should be in the guidance counselor's hands two weeks before the deadline date. (Chapters 8 and 9)

November

• If colleges require fall mid-semester or mid-quarter grades after your initial application, note this on the family calendar. It is your responsibility to get the necessary forms to your guidance counselor to have your grades sent to those colleges. *Do this at least 10 days in advance of the date set by the college.* It is also your responsibility to know when mid-semester grades are available and to let your teachers know, as a courtesy, that you need a grade at that time. (Chapters 8 and 10)

Date mid-semester grades available: ______________________________

College name: ______________________________

Date grades should be sent: ______________________________

College name: ____________________

Date grades should be sent: ____________________

College name: ____________________

Date grades should be sent: ____________________

College name: ____________________

Date grades should be sent: ____________________

• Check with the guidance office for financial aid forms and any further scholarship materials which may be available. (Chapters 11 and 14)

• Begin to fill out college application forms if you have not already done so. (Chapter 9)

• Review all "What's The Plan?" tasks. (Chapter 13)

• It's important to select and apply to a "safety school"—one at which you are 99% sure of being accepted. This is especially important if you are applying to competitive schools.

December

• Check college application deadlines for the months ahead. Make certain they are on the family calendar.

• Plan use of holiday break time to complete applications (if necessary) and to start financial aid forms. (Chapters 9 and 11) Financial aid forms are due as soon after Jan. 1 as possible.

• Review test dates to make sure all necessary tests have been completed.

January

• Financial aid forms should be completed as soon as possible.

• Check application deadline dates for February, March and April.

• Register for any further tests you may need in the guidance office.

• Take advantage of career exploration programs at your high school. Check in the guidance office for assistance. (Chapter 5)

February

• If a spring mid-semester/quarter grade report is required by a college, mark those dates on your calendar and get the forms to the guidance office 10 days ahead of time.

Date mid-semester grades available : ______________________

Date student requested they be sent : ______________________

Which colleges sent to : ______________________

____

• Check March and April application deadline dates. Give your guidance office at least two weeks to process your application. Remember, your college application is not the only one your counselor is handling at this time.

• Continue to research scholarships and other financial aid options. Do not overlook scholarships which may be offered by local organizations or businesses. (Chapters 11 and 14)

March

• This is a big month for application deadlines. Your applications should be in the guidance office as soon as possible.

• Any last minute campus visits should be taken now. (Chapter 10)

April

• When you are accepted by a college, note on your family calendar the deadline for notifying it whether you plan to accept. Note whether (and how much of) a deposit is necessary for confirmation of attendance. (Residence hall/dormitory housing may also require a confirmation.)

College name: ______________________________

Acceptance deadline date: ______________________________

Date deposit sent: ______________________________

Date housing confirmation returned: ______________________________

• It would be courteous to inform those colleges that have accepted you, but which you do not plan to attend, of your decision. It helps those admissions offices with their enrollment plans and may free up a space for someone else who is waiting.

May—September

• Read and keep all information sent to you by your college, even if it doesn't look important. Material is only sent once—keep everything in a file or in one drawer. It is important to set up your college record keeping system now!

• The next step is the Orientation session. This will be your opportunity to move smoothly into the college environment.

CHAPTER THIRTEEN

What's The Plan?

BOTH

INSTRUCTIONS: As a family, review each question and decide who will be responsible for each task relevant to your college search. Below each question, write the name(s) of the person(s) assigned each task. The student should do as many of these as possible.

1. Who will arrange and/or attend meetings with the high school counselor? For what purpose?

Name(s): ______________________________

Purpose: ______________________________

____

Date completed: ______________________________

2. Who will be responsible for scheduling course selections for high school?

Name(s): ____________________

Date completed: ____________________

3. Who will be responsible for record-keeping and filing? (This includes grades, health, extracurricular activities, sports, awards, jobs.)

Name(s): ____________________

4. Who will be responsible for obtaining a student transcript? (This includes class rank and grade point average information.)

Name(s): ____________________

Date completed: ____________________

5. Who will be responsible for the student's resume? Who will organize? Who will compose the rough draft? Who will type the final resume? Who will proofread? Who will arrange dropping it off and picking it up from the printer?

Organization by: ____________________

Date: ____________________

Rough draft by: ____________________

Date: ____________________

Typing by: ____________________

Date: ____________________

Proofreading by: ____________________

Date: ____________________

Printing by: ____________________

Date: ____________________

6. Who will be responsible for obtaining letters of recommendation and permission for recommendations?

Name(s): ____________________

COMPLETION RECORD

Letter requested from: ____________________

Date requested: ____________ Date received: ____________

Date(s) mailed to colleges: ____________________

Letter requested from: ____________________

Date requested: ____________ Date received: ____________

Date(s) mailed to colleges: ____________________

Letter requested from: ____________________

Date requested: ____________ Date received: ____________

Date(s) mailed to colleges: ____________________

Letter requested from: ____________________

Date requested: ____________ Date received: ____________

Date(s) mailed to colleges: ____________________

Letter requested from: ____________________

Date requested: ____________ Date received: ____________

Date(s) mailed to colleges: ____________________

7. Who will be responsible for setting up college shopping lists?

Name(s): ______________________________

First list completed (date): ______________________________

Revisions completed (dates): ______________________________

8. Who will schedule college visits, including admission office appointments?

Name(s): ______________________________

COMPLETION RECORD

College: ______________________________

Date visit scheduled: ______________________________

College: ______________________________

Date visit scheduled: ______________________________

College: ______________________________

Date visit scheduled: ______________________________

College: ______________________________

Date visit scheduled: ______________________________

College: ______________________________

Date visit scheduled: ______________________________

College: ______________________________

Date visit scheduled: ______________________________

9. Who will be responsible for obtaining application forms from colleges?

Name(s):______________________________

COMPLETION RECORD

College:______________________________

Date called/letter sent:______________________________

College:______________________________

Date called/letter sent:______________________________

College:______________________________

Date called/letter sent:______________________________

College:______________________________

Date called/letter sent:______________________________

College:______________________________

Date called/letter sent:______________________________

College:______________________________

Date called/letter sent:______________________________

10. Who will be responsible for researching application deadline dates? Who will enter them on the family calendar? (Be certain to mark dates when applications must go to guidance office in order to give counselors enough time to process them.)

Researched by:______________________________

Date:______________________________

Entered on calendar by:______________________________

Date: ______________________________

11. Who will proofread the application forms?

Name(s): ______________________________

COMPLETION RECORD

College: ______________________________

Date proofread: ______________________________

College: ______________________________

Date proofread: ______________________________

College: ______________________________

Date proofread: ______________________________

College: ______________________________

Date proofread: ______________________________

College: ______________________________

Date proofread: ______________________________

College: ______________________________

Date proofread: ______________________________

12. Who will type the final copy of each application form?

Name(s): ______________________________

COMPLETION RECORD

College: ______________________________

Date typed: ______________________________

College: ______________________________

Date typed: ______________________________

College: ______________________________

Date typed: ______________________________

College: ______________________________

Date typed: ______________________________

College: ______________________________

Date typed: ______________________________

College: ______________________________

Date typed: ______________________________

13. Who will make an "insurance" copy of each application and the accompanying check in case the application is lost? Be sure to file this information. Who will check with each school to make sure the application was received?

Name(s): ______________________________

COMPLETION RECORD

College: ______________________________

Date copy made: ______________ Received (date): ______________

College: ______________________________

Date copy made: ______________ Received (date): ______________

College: ______________________________

Date copy made: ______________ Received (date): ______________

College: ______________________________

Date copy made: ______________ Received (date): ______________

College: ______________________________

Date copy made: ______________ Received (date): ______________

College: ______________________________

Date copy made: ______________ Received (date): ______________

14. Who will attend the college fair in the autumn?

Name(s): ______________________________

15. Who will attend the financial aid information sessions offered at the college fair and at the high school?

Name(s): ______________________________

16. Who will send for financial aid forms from CSS and ACT? (These are available in January.)

Name(s): ______________________________

Date completed: ______________________________

17. Who will send for financial aid packets from the colleges?

Name(s): ______________________________

COMPLETION RECORD

College: ______________________________

Date information requested: ______________________________

College: ______________________________

Date information requested: ______________________________

College: ______________________________

Date information requested: ______________________________

College: ______________________________

Date information requested: ______________________________

College: ______________________________

Date information requested: ______________________________

College: ______________________________

Date information requested: ______________________________

18. Who will complete the family income tax forms?

Name(s): ______________________________

Date completed: ______________________________

19. Who will search for college scholarship materials:

At the public library? Name(s): ______________________________

At the bookstore? Name(s): ______________________________

At the colleges? Name(s): ______________________________

Where you work? Name(s): ______________________________

In the community (through organizations)? Name(s): ______________________________

Through your church/synagogue? Name(s) : ____________________

____

Through related professional organizations? Name(s) : ________

____

20. Who will check the deadlines for registration for PSAT, SAT, ACT and Achievement Tests? (NOTE: Remember that National Merit Scholarships are based on results of some of the tests!)

Name(s) : ______________________________________

Date(s) completed : ______________________________

21. Who will enter registration deadlines, actual test dates and locations on the calendar?

Name(s) : ______________________________________

Date(s) completed : ______________________________

22. Who will register for the PSAT, SAT, ACT and Achievement Tests in the guidance office and/or with the various testing services. (NOTE: Procedures for registration vary.)

Name(s) : ______________________________________

Date(s) completed : ______________________________

23. Who will make sure housing applications are in on time to colleges requiring them?

Name(s) : ______________________________________

Date completed : _________________________________

CHAPTER FOURTEEN

Resource List

The following list suggests additional resources you may wish to consult as you continue your college planning. We have included books. computer programs and videos and segmented them by topic. Entries marked with an asterisk (*) are particularly recommended.

BOOKS

Applications

*Curry, B., Ed., **Essays That Work: 50 Essays from Successful Applications to the Nation's Top Colleges.** New Haven, CT: Mustang Publications, 1986.

Van Raalte, S. D., **Apply Yourself: Writing College Applications That Get Results.** New York: Fawcett Columbine, 1985.

Athlete's Information

Callahan, T. R., **Callahan's College Guide to Athletics and Academics in America.** New York: Harper and Row, 1984.

*Figler, S. and Figler, H., **The Athlete's Game Plan for College and Career.** Princeton, NJ: Peterson's Guides, 1984.

Green, B. and Green, A., **The Directory of Athletic Scholarships.** New York: G. P. Putnam's Sons, 1981

__________, **High School Planning for College Bound Athletes.** Skokie, IL: National Association of College Admissions Counselors, 1986.

Career Guidance

Baldrige, L., **Letitia Baldrige's Complete Guide to Executive Manners.** New York: Rawson Associates, 1985.

Cetron, M. J., **Jobs of the Future: The 500 Best Jobs and Where They'll Be and How to Get Them.** New York: McGraw-Hill Book Co, 1984.

*Fry, Ronald W. (ed.), **1987 Advertising Career Directory.** Hawthorne, NJ: The Career Press, 1987.

*Fry, Ronald W. (ed.), **1987 Book Publishing Career Directory.** Hawthorne, NJ: The Career Press, 1987.

*Fry, Ronald W. (ed.), **1987 Magazines Career Directory.** Hawthorne, NJ: The Career Press, 1987.

*Fry, Ronald W. (ed.), **1987 Marketing and Sales Career Directory.** Hawthorne, NJ: The Career Press, 1987.

*Fry, Ronald W. (ed.), **1987 Newspapers Career Directory.** Hawthorne, NJ: The Career Press, 1987.

*Fry, Ronald W. (ed.), **1987 Public Relations Career Directory.** Hawthorne, NJ: The Career Press, 1987.

NOTE: Above six books are part of annual Career Directory Series. Be sure to request most recent update (and information on new volumes).

Gale, B. and Gale, L., **Discover What You're Best At: The National Career Aptitude Test.** New York: Simon and Schuster, 1982.

Nadler, B. J., **Liberal Arts Jobs.** Princeton, NJ: Peterson's Guides, 1986.

*Snelling, A. M. and Snelling, R. O., Jr., **Jobs: What They Are, Where They Are, What They Pay.** New York: Simon and Schuster, 1985.

College Shopping

___________, **Barron's Profiles of American Colleges.** Woodbury, NY: Barron's Educational Series, Inc., 1982.

Cass, James and Birnbaum, Max., **The Comparative Guide to American Colleges.** New York: Harper & Row, 1985.

*Fiske, E. B., **Selective Guide to Colleges.** New York: Times Books, 1983.

Hegener, K. C., Ed., **Peterson's Competitive Colleges.** Princeton, NJ: Peterson's Guides, 1985.

___________, **Index of Majors: 1986-87.** New York: College Entrance Examination Board, 1986.

*McClintock, J., **One Hundred Top Colleges: How to Choose and Get In.** New York: Wiley Press, 1982.

*McQuaid, P., **How to Get Into An Ivy League School.** New York: Monarch Press, 1985.

*Moll, R., **The Public Ivys: A Guide to America's Best State Colleges and Universities.** New York: Viking Penguin, Inc., 1986.

____________, **The College Handbook.** New York: College Entrance Examination Board, 1986.

*The Yale Daily News Staff, **The Insider's Guide to the Colleges.** New York: G. P. Putnam Sons, 1986.

Financial Aid

Brownstone, D. M. and Hawes, G. R., **The College Money Book: How to Get a High Quality Education at the Lowest Possible Cost.** New York: Bobbs Merrill, 1984.

College Scholarship Service of the College Board., **The College Cost Book: 1986-1987.** New York: The College Entrance Examination Board, 1985.

Lehman, A. E. and Suber, E. A., **The College Money Handbook: The Complete Guide to Expenses, Scholarships, Loans, Jobs, and Special Programs at Four-Year Colleges.** Princeton: NJ: Peterson's Guides, 1985.

*Leider, R. and Leider, A., **Don't Miss Out: The Ambitious Student's Guide to Financial Aid, 1987-1988.** New York: Simon and Schuster, 1985.

*Schlachter, Gail Ann, **Directory of Financial Aids for Minorites 1986-1987.** Redwood City, CA: Reference Service Press, 1986.

*Schlachter, Gail Ann, **Directory of Financial Aids for Women 1987-1988.** Redwood City, CA: Reference Service Press, 1987.

*Schlachter, Gail Ann, **How to Find Out About Financial Aid: A Guide to Over 700 Directories.** Redwood City, CA: Reference Service Press, 1987.

Resume Preparation

*Fry, Ronald W., **Your First Resume: A step-by-step approach for resume and cover letter preparation for high school and college students.** Hawthorne, NJ: The Career Press, 1987.

*Krannich, Ronald L. and Banis, William J., **High Impact Resumes & Letters (2nd edition)**. Manassas, VA: Impact Publications, 1987.

Testing

Bobrow, P. J., et. al., **Cliff's The American College Testing Preparation Guide.** Lincoln, NE: Cliff's Notes, 1986.

Brownstein, S. C., Weiner, M., and Green, S. W., **Barron's How to Prepare for the SAT (14th edition).** Woodbury, NY: Barron's Educational Series, Inc., 1987.

Divine, J. H. and Kylen, D. W., **How to Beat Test Anxiety and Score Higher on the SAT and All Other Exams.** Woodbury, New York: Barron's Educational Series, Inc., 1982.

Shapiro, M. (ed.), **Barron's ACT.** Woodbury, NY: Barron's Educational Series, Inc., 1985.

COMPUTER SOFTWARE

The following programs are available for most personal computers (Apple, IBM, etc.). Unlike books or videos, computer programs are designed to give you personalized feedback on *your* progress or needs. Software is more expensive than books, so look for these recommended titles in your high school guidance office or borrow them from your library (or even a private college consultant).

Applications

College Entry. New York: The College Board, 1986.

Career Guidance

Careers of the Future. Vancouver, WA: Careers of the Future, 1984.

***Discover for Microcomputers: A Computer Based Career Guidance System.** Hunt Valley, MD: American College Testing, 1986.

College Shopping

Advanced Placement Explorer. New York: The College Board, 1986.

College Decision. Houston, TX: Educational Planning, 1985.

***Peterson's College Selection Service: Four-Year Colleges.** Princeton, NJ: Peterson's Guides, Inc., 1987.

Financial Aid

***Scholarships Today.** Charleston, WV: Jefferson Software, 1986.

Testing

Barron's Computer Study Program for the SAT. Woodbury, NY: Barron's, 1986.

***Test Sense: Preparing for the PSAT/NMSQT.** New York: The College Board, 1985.

VIDEOS

If you have found that you like to learn by watching, videos may be the answer for you. They can also help in college shopping as a preview to an actual campus visit. Again, videos are much more costly, so try to borrow or rent them.

College Shopping

Laser Disc College Choice Center. Durham, NC: Learning Resources Network, 1986. (Each video about a college is 5-10 minutes long.)

*Vlandis, J. W. & Nieuwenhaus, M. A., **The College Interview.** Westport, CT: Educational Visions, 1985. (38 minutes).

Testing

***The Video SAT Review.** Westminster, MD: Random House Video, 1985. (2 hours).

EPILOGUE

Our best advice to you is to be understanding with each other and to enjoy one another during these hectic months of planning. Try to dispel your sense of failure if or when that first rejection notice arrives. It may seem devastating at the time, but it will probably work out for the best in the long run. And don't forget to celebrate when that first acceptance comes!

Through our own experiences and our college planning workshops, we know first-hand that the future does arrive sooner than you think. The moment came when Bonnie was about to leave her son to start his first year of college. They laughed and congratulated each other on making it through the process.

As she put her arms around this grown college freshman to say good-by, she was surprised to find that she was crying. But her son's reaction surprised (and heartened) her even more: "Mom, it's okay," he smiled. "If you didn't cry now I wouldn't think you cared." Another phase had begun.

Good luck on your own new phases, students and parents alike.

IF YOU NEED MORE WORKSHEETS, WE CAN HELP:

WORKSHEET BOOKLET

COLLEGE COMES SOONER THAN YOU THINK!

While we've attempted to make **College Comes Sooner Than You Think!** eminently practical and easy-to-use, we know there are families out there who will need more forms...or just more room to write.

So, through a special co-publishing arrangement with Grolier Educational Corporation, we have extracted all the forms a family might need —even added extra copies of those we expect will get the most use—and printed them in a separate, 8 1/2 x 11, 64-page **Worksheet Booklet**.

This Booklet is available only through high school guidance counselors (who, in turn, should order from the Select Library Division of Grolier). So if your family needs more room and/or more forms, ask your high school guidance counselor for a copy of this convenient Worksheet Booklet! (And if they don't have any, ask them to call either Grolier—1-800-243-7256—or the Career Press —1-800-CAREER-1—to order them.)

INDEX

D

E

F

P,Q

R

S

T

U

V

W

X,Y,Z

NOTES